Saintly Enigma

To Pennar's children – Rhiannon, Geraint, Owain and Hywel and their families, and grandson Gwri. In loving memory of Meirion (1944–2010), and to my family – Delyth, Lythan and Phil, Hywel, Emrys and Carys, Dafydd and Mandy and to all those former students, ministers of Word and Sacraments who benefitted so much from Pennar's ministry

Saintly Enigma

A biography of

Pennar Davies

Ivor Thomas Rees

Ivor Thomas Rees

y**L**olfa

First impression: 2011

© Copyright Ivor Thomas Rees and Y Lolfa Cyf., 2011

The contents of this book are subject to copyright, and may
not be reproduced by any means, mechanical or electronic,
without the prior, written consent of the publishers.

Cover design: Y Lolfa
Cover photograph: courtesy of Pennar Davies's family

ISBN: 978 184771 370 4

FSC

Published and printed in Wales
on paper from well maintained forests
by Y Lolfa Cyf., Talybont, Ceredigion SY24 5HE
website www.ylolfa.com
e-mail ylolfa@ylolfa.com
tel 01970 832 304
fax 832 782

Contents

Foreword

ON THE CENTENARY of his birth it is excellent to see a renewed interest in the life and work of that remarkable literary and spiritual figure Pennar Davies coming to the fore. With Herbert Hughes's translation of Pennar's classic on the spiritual life, *Cudd fy Meiau* [Cover my sins] about to appear as *The Diary of a Soul* replete with an insightful preface by the Archbishop of Canterbury, it is both a pleasure and a privilege to commend this succinct and lively biography by Ivor Thomas Rees. Each work conveys not only the respect and appreciation of two men much indebted to the testimony of a unique individual, but they afford a glimpse into the genius of one of twentieth-century Wales' most extraordinary sons.

In one way it is difficult to appreciate Pennar's contribution, as the Wales which bred him, and to which he gave his life, has by now practically disappeared. The hardship of the Glamorganshire valleys between the two world wars, an almost transcendent faith in education as a way of betterment, the unquestioned assumptions of conventional morality and organized religion in everyday life, and the appeal – at least for some – of a vibrant, transformational personal faith, belong to a world which is receding rapidly into the past. With devolved government a fact and the Welsh language afforded official status, would Pennar and his contemporaries like Gwynfor Evans, J Gwyn Griffiths, R Tudur Jones and others, recognize the new Wales for which they strove and yearned? With Welsh Nonconformity itself a thing of the past, as a significant social movement at least, and Welsh language culture hugely secularized, how, one wonders, would they respond? The vision which spurs a generation on, often with self-sacrificial zeal, rarely results in the reality which was imagined, but the vision itself can retain its integrity even in a new and radically different world.

This being said, Pennar's work can be enjoyed anew, not because of its context – though everything he wrote and did was deeply contextualized – but because of its intrinsic value both literary and spiritual. For those who can access his work, Pennar's novels, his short stories, his criticism and essays, will long retain their value, while some of his poetry is sublime. Though still neglected, his 'Cathl i'r Almonwydden' [A hymn to the almond tree] from the 1961 volume *Yr Efrydd o Lyn Cynon* [The cripple from the vale of Cynon] can be compared with Waldo Williams' 'Mewn Dau Gae' [In two fields] as one of the most striking Welsh poems of the postwar generation. His English-language scholarship can still be read with profit, but surely it is his spiritual notebook *Cudd Fy Meiau* which is the classic. A deeply spiritual writer, who, despite his somewhat unorthodox Pelagianism, was rooted in the wonder of the New Testament Christ, the book conveys the pain and the glory of the inner life with profound sensitivity and astonishing perception. For Pennar, as for Gwenallt and Euros Bowen, two other Christian poets of his generation, all truth is incarnate truth, and while the context of *Cudd Fy Meiau* is the uneventful life of a Welsh Nonconformist minister and academic in the drab 1950s, the content is universal. Like Herbert Hughes, Ivor Thomas Rees was a student of Pennar's when the volume first appeared in weekly instalments in *Y Tyst* [The witness], the newspaper of the Welsh Congregationalists, and his recollections of college life in Brecon convey not only Nonconformity having to face squarely the crisis of the time, but describe Pennar's influence – and sometimes his foibles – on those among whom he laboured and lived.

Although I only met Pennar Davies once, at the examination board of the University of Wales's Faculty of Theology in Shrewsbury in 1988 when I was in my first year as an academic and Pennar in his last, it was an enormous pleasure to prepare a Welsh language biography which appeared in 2003, six years after he had passed away. This book both supplements my own and provides those who have no Welsh with a vivid portrait of a good and remarkable man.

D Densil Morgan
University of Wales Trinity St David
February 2011

Dad

LATE IN 2010, I lost my eldest brother suddenly. Meirion's death was a great blow to us all as a family. I feel his loss in many different ways every day, but I missed him particularly as I read Rev. Ivor Rees' lively biography of my father's life.

As the eldest son, Meirion was closer than the rest of us five children to the young Pennar Davies, the one I never came to know. By the time I, as the 'cyw melyn olaf' (the spoilt youngest child) remember him, he was most certainly middle-aged. Grey-haired and balding, I dubbed him 'heni' (oldie) at one point in my cheeky teens – much to his bemusement. I never asked him whether calling him by this name or another nickname, 'moelyn' (baldie), ever hurt him. He usually just smiled at me. He hardly ever raised his voice at his baby 'Bw' (my childhood nickname); he left the disciplinary hearings to my rather more sharp-eyed, stricter, most certainly Germanic mother.

Neither of us five children of course remembers the Davies, Aberpennar or the William Thomas Davies who lived largely through the English language and was a self-confessed agnostic. Some aspects of my father's inner spiritual life during Oxford and Yale days will remain forever a mystery. However, the elder three – the Brecon three as I call them – Meirion, Rhiannon and Geraint – were nearer to the younger man than Hywel and I.

This Pennar Davies would often come to the fore suddenly in a sharp, witty, almost scathing, comment about certain people. The victims were often ambitious British-centric Welsh politicians, of which there were plenty in the 1960s and 1970s.

Underneath the loving and serene Pennar Davies, there was

a little bit of the roguish humour, which you can detect in his work.

Meirion, who'd worked closest with 'Sgipi' (another nickname for my father) on creative projects, witnessed more of this wit than the rest of us. But all five of us tasted some snippets of this somewhat mischievous humour.

Some of the diaries that I read from his days at Yale showed a very sharp wit, later also seen in some of his Welsh writings. His life among the postgraduates of Yale must have felt a million miles away from his impoverished childhood in Mountain Ash. He had been on a long journey.

His journey had been quite an eventful one spiritually too, as he travelled far in his personal Christian pilgrimage. Maybe because of his eclectic interests, his theology seemed to take him sometimes to the boundaries of the Christian faith. He would talk to us more about the human Jesus than the risen Christ and the spirit within us rather than the spirit at work in real historic events.

His theology seemed to combine the doer praised in the book of James and mysticism more akin to some of the Far Eastern religions. However, when I once asked him in a challenging fashion whether he believed in angels, he said he did because "the impossible was sometimes believable". The point is this – he came very close to the boundaries of faith but never crossed them.

For us children, he left a curious legacy. We all understood the importance of Jesus and Christianity but his questioning mind made us doubt and question. This was evident in my brother Meirion's work whose poems and beliefs were often, to coin a phrase of my father's, "between myth and creed".

However, what we will remember more than anything else about dad was his love, care and passion for us, his children and for our mother. Of course, it was Mam who shouldered most of the responsibilities for the day-to-day running of the home and family, but Dad loved having us children around him. He always had time to kiss, cuddle and talk to us, even when we must have tested his patience. I was forever on his lap as he typed on his Erika typewriter or wrote notes in miniscule style in notebooks or pieces of paper. The joy of fatherhood – which spanned many years because of the huge gap between first-born and last-born – often inspired him in his writings.

One of my most precious childhood memories is a moment he captured in my life in his poem 'Disgyrchiant' (Gravity). It was an incident I would never have remembered if it hadn't been for the poem. 'Disgyrchiant' talks about the time when, as a nine year old in 1970, I gave the thumbs up to an Asian passing on the street. In this little piece of childhood action, he saw a uniting of different worlds, the gravity bringing together different cultures. That was Dad through and through – seeing the spiritual in everyday human endeavour.

Sometimes he over-romanticised man's ability to improve his lot and uphold the highest moral standards under the guidance of God. He was certainly like that with us children, believing that we could achieve goals sometimes beyond us. But that was a reflection of his belief and faith in us – a love that we, as his four remaining children, will cherish forever.

Owain Pennar
Cardiff
March 2011

Preface

THE PUBLICATION OF Pennar Davies' magnificent biography by Professor Densil Morgan was warmly welcomed by Welsh readers, among whom was this former student at Coleg Coffa. The reaction of non-Welsh speaking colleagues, in particular, the Rev. Malcolm Page (1938–2010) to my enthusiasm, was to demand that I should translate it into English. With the author's gracious consent I began but, on completing two chapters, I realised that such a task would be a great drain on my limited resources, and so I decided to embark on a smaller work, though still using Professor Morgan's volume as a major source of information and insight. Added to this, of course, are my own recollections of my three years at Brecon and the relationship between the college principal and myself, as well as many conversations with friends and colleagues. November 2011 marks the centenary of the birth of Pennar Davies and, as no one else to my knowledge, has taken up the biographer's pen to write of him in English, I offer this work to help mark the occasion.

It is necessary that I note my gratitude to all who have encouraged me in this task and especially those who have contributed to the volume from their own point of view. Professor Densil Morgan has been gracious, both in his support and, with the University of Wales Press, in allowing me to quote in translation from his Welsh biography of Pennar Davies. Dr Meic Stephens too is to be thanked for permitting me to quote both from *Artists in Wales* and his obituary in *The Independent*. Thanks must go to the Llanelli Reference Library and the National Library of Wales. Delyth, my wife, must be thanked for her customary support and general help, as well as for using her gift of proofreading. My debt of gratitude to Mr Heini Gruffudd for his outstanding help, advice and constant encouragement is indeed great; he supplied a number of photographs also. Thanks go to Mr Owain Pennar for reading the manuscript and providing valuable information, as well as arranging for the translation of his father's poem 'A Hymn to the Almond Tree' and to Mr Hywel Pennar for supplying family photographs. I am indebted to the members of Pennar's family for their encouragement and their generous gift in memory of their mother Rosemarie Pennar Davies. Thanks are due also to those bodies which, by their generosity, have made the publication possible: the National Synod of Wales of the United Reformed Church, through its Osborne Trust; the Marquis Trust (URC History Society and Westminster College, Cambridge); Mansfield College, Oxford, the Congregational Library and the Congregational History Society. Last but not least my thanks go to Gwasg y Lolfa and especially Mr Lefi Gruffudd and Ms Eirian Jones.

Except where it is otherwise stated, all translations from Welsh to English in this work are the result of my poor efforts.

Ivor Thomas Rees
Swansea
St David's Day 2011

14

1

A Gentle Welsh Giant

FEW ACADEMICS DELIBERATELY turn from the university ladder to fame and few scholars reject the opportunity to take centre stage in their field of excellence. Only a minority of people set aside preferment, success as well as personal comfort to pursue a vision. One such person was William Thomas Pennar Davies. Pennar Davies did not become a leading figure in the realms of English literature as a writer, a poet and a scholar. Indeed, he is virtually unknown outside Welsh-speaking circles. This is due to a deliberate choice on his part to sacrifice all of the above in order to take his place in the struggle to save the Welsh language and culture. For the same reason his name is hardly known in church circles outside Welsh-speaking Nonconformity and that is also a great loss to everyone. So who was this man, described by his Welsh biographer D Densil Morgan as "a unique figure in the recent history of Wales... a man of God who was also a great writer"? The phrase "man of God" was used also by Gwynfor Evans, prominent Welsh Congregationalist and former leader of Plaid Cymru. Many people have described Pennar as enigmatic, whilst his friend from his student days, and prominent historian of English Congregationalism, Dr Geoffrey Nuttall, described him thus: "His personality was unlike no one else's. I could call it enigmatic... but I prefer to say *complexion oppositorum (a union of opposites)...* Discussion left me sure there was a strong unity in him, embracing the puzzling opposites. If only I could find it, but I never did... Dear Pennar keeps us guessing... I can hear his chuckle still."[1]

Pennar Davies, a giant in the cultural, political and religious life of Wales in the twentieth century, lived through nine of its ten decades. As a young man he experienced the dire poverty of the south Wales mining valleys in the years after the Great War – and a community which honoured scholarship and education both for its own sake as a means of escape from the dire social circumstances. After being educated at the local elementary and county schools and three universities (Wales, Oxford (twice) and Yale), this polymath could have become a leading scholar in the field of English literature or in world Congregationalism, making his name as a writer and a teacher in English Literature at the University of Wales or Church History at Oxford University. Instead he turned his back on academic success and its accompanying honours in order to serve his own people and his religious faith in a poverty more genteel and less acute than that of his parents, but real and painful nonetheless. Coming from a non-Welsh-speaking home, he became a major contributor to Welsh language and literature as poet, critic, novelist and writer. His decision to write almost only in this minority tongue, in token of his commitment to save the language and the culture of Wales, meant that he chose deliberately to sacrifice both world renown and financial reward, which would doubtless have been his had he used English, of which he was such a master.

Growing up in a society whose chief concern with the class struggle, he became a leading figure in Plaid Cymru, seeking to unite all Welsh people in the struggle for national consciousness and freedom. The son of a former professional soldier, he espoused the pacifist cause with passion. Coming from a family where, despite his mother's efforts, religion did not have a central place, he followed a path which led from early conversion to agnosticism, if not atheism, then a second conversion when faced with the inhumanity and barbarism threatening Europe and the world in the late 1930s. This led him to train for the Christian ministry, where he was ordained and served a local church, and later went on to play a leading role in church life in Wales by helping train young men and women to follow a similar vocation.

2

Mountain Ash (Aberpennar) 1911–34

PENNAR DAVIES, ALTHOUGH unique in so many ways, was a typical son of the south Wales mining valleys of his generation and the next. He was born into poverty and his family on both sides had migrated from rural Wales. To try and understand this man it is necessary to know something of the "rock from which he was hewn".[1]

The valleys of Glamorgan and Monmouthshire were a veritable Yukon from the 1850s to the outbreak of the Great War. People poured in from the rest of Wales and across Offa's Dyke, from Ireland and Europe. It is said that the rate of immigration into Wales during this period was second only to that of the United States. Among them were the Welsh Baptists, Joseph and Margaret Davies, from the Preseli hills of north Pembrokeshire. They arrived at Mountain Ash (Aberpennar), where the river Pennar met the river Cynon before that joined the river Taff at Abercynon. One of their sons, William, a young founder of a Baptist chapel, made two girls pregnant at around the same time. He was persuaded to marry Jane, who died giving birth to their son, Joseph (Little Jo). Jo was packed off to his mother's cousin at Trealaw in the Rhondda valley, whilst his father then married the other girl, Ann Sage, who by now had given birth to William junior. As the years went by, drink became more important than the Baptist cause and the situation worsened after the death of his wife. From then on he alternated between the homes of his two sons, Joseph and William. Pennar describes him as a "ragged and coarse drunkard".[2]

> Before his condition deteriorated so grievously he would look with some gentle pride on his grandchildren but he became increasingly careless of his personal hygiene until lice could be seen adorning his jacket. When he stayed at our house there was no place for him to sleep apart from my bed, and his breath was so full of alcohol that I would be rather drunk getting up in the morning.[3]

A place was then found for him in a local lodging house, where he remained until taken to a mental hospital in Bridgend. "He went there cursing his offspring"[4] but his children visited him faithfully until his death in 1925.

Little Jo, a small, dark man, later to be Pennar's father, received loving care from his foster parents. He was steeped in Calvinistic Methodist values. He taught himself the piano and mastered tonic sol-fa, enabling him to play hymn tunes for the rest of his life. Jo was weary of the restrictions of his Calvinistic Methodist home, where life became even more confined after his foster father was killed in a colliery explosion. Jo fled to Cardiff where he joined the Welch Regiment, taking delight in later years in the fact that he had served three English monarchs – Victoria, Edward VII and George V. Jo was fiercely proud of the fact that he served in the army, especially as it showed how fearless the Welsh were. Pennar remarked on more than one occasion that it was his father's pride in being a Welshman in the British army which made his son a Welsh patriot from an early age, and later a Welsh nationalist. It is strange to think that his father's career as a soldier had such a profound effect on a young man who later became such a convinced pacifist.

Jo would spend his leave, not in Trealaw, but in Mountain Ash, with either of his half-siblings, Billy and Besi. During one of these leaves of absence, on a visit to nearby Pontypridd, he set eyes on Edith Ann Moss from Hirwaun, near Aberdare.

They fell in love. Jo left the army to become a coal miner and they were married at Pontypridd Registry Office in 1902.

Whereas Edith's family, like that of Joseph, hailed from Pembrokeshire, she was from the Englishry[5] in the south of the county, having been born at Haverfordwest in 1880. Her parents, William Henry and Bessie Moss, moved to Aberdare in 1885, leaving Edith in the care of her grandparents; but all three joined her parents in 1888. In 1892, the Moss family, now with three children, settled at Hirwaun. Her grandparents had a house nearby and Edith moved to and fro between the two homes. The language, culture, religion and outlook of the Moss family were English and Anglican. To them the Hirwaun folk culture was coarse and vulgar and "it was there that my mother learned to hate the Welsh people and their language".[6] Marrying into Jo's family did little to lessen her anti-Welsh prejudices. "After she married my father and came to live among his people, she was confirmed in this opinion by discovering that her in-laws were not as clean, respectable or temperate as she had expected. Her hopes for a comfortable, inoffensive and respectable family life vanished in one evening." Entering her husband's community must have been a terrible shock for the newly wedded bride and an affront to her sense of social superiority. Nothing had prepared her for "the unfettered paganism of these coalminers".

Jo and Edith rented a terraced house, 11 Duffryn Street, Mountain Ash. Both house and street were bleak and poor. It was in this two-up, two-down, with small kitchen, cellar and outside toilet that their three daughters and one son were born and raised. Edith Jessie (Jess) born in 1905, was the first; she had a lovely singing voice and inherited her father's interest in music; she eventually married Cliff Maddern, a local lad, whose roots were in Somerset. Then came Doris May (Dol), with whom Pennar had a special relationship in childhood; her husband would be Alf Binding, whose family also came from Somerset. Edith gave birth to her son, William Thomas, on 12 November 1911; like Dol, he resembled his mother in appearance and colouring more than his father. In his article 'Cychwyn' [Beginning] in the July 1988 issue of the magazine *Taliesin*, Pennar imagines the situation at 11 Duffryn Street, Mountain Ash, on 12 November 1911, when his parents were trying to decide on a name for their newly-born: His non-Welsh-speaking mother says to her husband, "I still want to name him Merlin – Merlin Miles – Merlin Miles Davies – it sounds very nice." His Welsh-speaking father replies, "I don't like grand names. It's tempting providence. Give him a good old Welsh name – William Thomas." And his father had his way.

Finally, Florence Graham (Floss) arrived in 1914; she left home to go into service, before marrying Walter Scott and moving to Hull. There can be no doubt whatsoever of Pennar's great affection for his sisters, with whom he kept in touch throughout his life: "I can say with complete confidence that the relationship between us in our old home was loving and kind."[7] The Davies family shared in the grinding poverty of the south Wales mining valleys of the period. Pennar described his childhood in *Artists in Wales*: "Our family politics were ready-made; we were in the class struggle. It was not so much 'ideology' as hunger: threadbare shabbiness and horror of the debt collector. Half a boiled egg was rare enough to be a treat."[8]

Pennar was unique in the family at 11 Duffryn Street: his parents and sisters were ordinary working class folk, with no pretence at intellectual skills and it was soon apparent that "our little Willie", studious and dreamy, was 'different'. That difference was further accentuated when he learnt Welsh: "Later on, after hearing that I spoke Welsh and had begun publishing books in that strange tongue, they came to the conclusion that there was more than one kind of madness."[9] The whole family agreed that Willie should not follow his father into the mines. Jo's own hatred of his occupation grew as the years went by: "My father was a little man, sensitive, jocular, genial, remarkably affectionate in his good moods, but with a fear of the dangers of his daily work in the coal mine."[10] After turning his back on the chapel, Jo's culture became English in outlook and secular, but he still spoke the Welsh dialect he had learned in the Rhondda, and represented Welshness in the family. He took pride in his regiment, saying "stick it, the Welch" when troubled by toothache or any other ailment. His two delights were choral music and boxing. He sang the praises of Cardiff's 'Peerless' Jim Driscoll[11] and claimed to be related to Pontypridd's Freddie Welsh,[12] the British lightweight boxing champion. His twin loyalties were to the Crown and the Labour movement, but he came to quietly delight in his son's increasing Welshness.

Edith stated that she was English. She was the moral authority in the household. A strong bond developed between the mother and her son, who said of her that "my mother was tender, conscientious and devoted".[13] "I was my mother's son."[14] Among the other words he used to describe her were "meek, quiet, kind, dignified, genteel and suffering". Brought up an Anglican, she was unable to attend the local parish church because of family commitments. After several years she came to feel that her young children should grow up in the knowledge of God.[15] The children had been attending the Sunday school at Capel y Ffrwd, the Baptist church of which their grandfather was a founder, and where Pennar had learned the Welsh alphabet, but she transferred them to Providence English Congregational Church, which was only a couple of hundred yards from their home. Edith herself began to worship there; her name appeared in the subscribers' list from 1922 onward, and she became a church member soon afterwards. Willie Davies' name was first listed in 1923. Jo refused to have anything to do with chapel of any kind. This was part of the tension in the family's life which surfaced from time to time, despite the genuine affection and love which each parent had for the other. Pennar himself returned more than once in his writing to this theme:

It must be admitted for the sake of truth that there was too much quarrelling between my parents. My father's wages were small and his work as an underground miner tremendously dangerous. My father was popular among his workmates and enjoyed his popularity. He hated to refuse to go to a pub with some 'friend', and it was often the case that he paid for the friend's beer as well as his own. His great popularity among his fellow miners was gained at the expense of his family... They were a dear couple, and my chief sorrow as a child was to hear and see the heart-breaking clashes between them.[16]

But Jo was not the only source of worry and shame for Edith: despite her efforts to keep them 'on the straight and narrow' all three 'had to marry', thus robbing their mother of her desire for each to have a respectable wedding. Despite this, all three sons-in-law were warmly welcomed into the family and, as far as their brother could tell, all three couples lived happily together. However, Pennar's biographer, D Densil Morgan, comments, "considering the frequency of these unfortunate events and the history of the wider family, it is little wonder that the place of the flesh and its relationship to the spirit should become one of the themes of the older Pennar's most serious meditation".[17]

As was usual in the south Wales valleys, certainly up to the end of World War II, Pennar[18] began his schooling at Duffryn Infants School in 1914, when he was three years old, moving up to the Boys School two years later. These were among his happiest years and in his old age he would recall with pleasure playing marbles, cowboys and indians, and 'jackie and doggie' (a valley game played with two sticks) and collecting cigarette cards. He passed the scholarship examination to Mountain Ash County School in 1922, coming top. There he remained for the next seven years, a continuous nightmare for this pale, delicate looking boy, the apple of his doting mother's eye, who stood out at school because he was taller than most of his fellow pupils. He retained the top place in his form in every examination but failed hopelessly in every sporting activity. The malicious use of the terms 'swot' and 'pasty face' caused him great pain. "I was pale and my movements were awkward; I was the object of constant mockery and bullying."[19] Whilst his time at the county school provided him with the foundation for his future academic success it did nothing for the development of his social skills. It was at the county school that his interest in Welsh was fostered and developed. By the fifth form Pennar was able to read his father tongue with ease and could write correctly and well, but lacked the confidence to speak it. In his Higher School Certificate (A level) he obtained the highest grades in Welsh, Latin and English. His school books show the breadth of his reading and the knowledge it gave him of Shakespeare and other writers in English, classical Greek drama in translation and several Welsh poets – no small feat for a boy from his family and social background.

Throughout his early teens Pennar was faithful at Providence Congregational Church, both in the Sunday school and at worship.[20] He was not baptised as a child. He confided to his students at Brecon in the 1950s that he had decided to ask one of them to baptise him but changed his mind when some other denominations issued statements declaring it to be essential. However, he believed that he had been "baptised once with the Risen Christ", referring to a conversion experience he underwent under the ministry of an English evangelist named Barraclough, who held a mission at Providence.

> When I was about twelve I received a kind of religious conversion. A zealous preacher, leading a spiritual revival at Providence Chapel, was able to present his message in a most gripping way. I was far from being the only member who responded to his message with enthusiasm. The full meaning of the word 'gospel' came home to me as good news of great joy.

In 'Clawr Coch' he describes the occasion:

> About twenty of us got up and joined each other in the space between the pulpit and the big seat.[21] We received a welcome and a blessing there and the preacher came down from the pulpit to shake us by the hand. I was the youngest of those returning [to the faith] and he drew attention to this when shaking my hand.

But was I too young to experience such guilt... I have been long disillusioned by this kind of conversion, but I can forget neither the value of the effect of the experience upon me nor the words of the preacher to me, spoken in the presence of the congregation: 'Give the soul to the Father who created it and the Son who died for it.'

One direct result of this conversion was the willingness of the young lad to proclaim his faith. His papers contain several references to the Providence prayer meeting. He himself refers to his venturing into public prayer, and soon it was being suggested that he should consider training for the ministry. However, by the time Pennar was giving serious thought to his career, his faith was being weakened by the works of T H Huxley[22] and he came to regard traditional religion as superstition and religious experience as psychological rather than spiritual in essence. In its turn, his atheism was replaced by a kind of romantic pantheism, which he called 'bywyaeth' (lifeism). He was aware of the mystery of creation and searched for the meaning of life but, even if he so desired, he was never able to deny his upbringing and the experiences of his youth at Providence, and it was to Providence that he ultimately returned years later when he rediscovered his faith and put forward his candidature for the ministry.

3

Academia, Welsh and English

University College, Cardiff 1929–34

IN 1929 PENNAR Davies became an undergraduate at the University College of South Wales and Monmouthshire, Cardiff, a constituent college of the University of Wales, reading Latin, English and Welsh. The scholarship he won was for sixty pounds a year but this was far from enough to pay for tuition fees and lodgings in the city. So, like many other students from the coal mining valleys, he had to live at home and take the train to Cardiff each day. His studies, accompanied by wide reading, left him little time for socialising. In his notes he speaks of a number of young men who reached prominence in later life, but the most important new friendship was that with John Gwyn Griffiths,[1] son of a Rhondda Baptist minister, and a student in the Classics, who ultimately persuaded him to converse in Welsh, when in a punt on Oxford's river Cherwell. Griffiths later married a German Egyptologist, Dr Käthe Bosse,[2] and it was they who introduced Pennar to a young German lady, Rosemarie Wolff, who later became his wife.

To the disappointment of the Professor of Welsh, Griffith John Williams, Pennar decided to concentrate on Classics, and both he and Gwyn Griffiths obtained Firsts in Latin in 1932. A year later Pennar gained another First, this time in English. There followed a happy and interesting year training to be a teacher. He was sent to two very different Cardiff schools, Stacey Road Boys' School, Splott, where he taught a wide range of subjects, and Cathays High School. He did very well in the theoretical part of his course and enjoyed mastering the social principles of education and child psychology. As to his performance in class, his tutor commented, "Try to be brisker and more forceful in your exposition and questioning... You should also look to your discipline... You are somewhat too retiring in disposition."[3] He later admitted to his family that he was never a natural school teacher and that discipline in the classroom was never his strong point.

Throughout this period Pennar lived in two worlds – the one at Cardiff and its university, and the other with his family in the poverty of Mountain Ash. Despite his agnosticism he continued to attend Providence, where he appreciated the ministry of the Rev. D Garro-Jones. At this time, however, it was poetry in English and increasingly in Welsh, rather than religion, which drew his attention:

To our forefathers, religion was intensely and gloriously a spiritual thing. To men God was a spirit, and they worshipped him in spirit and in truth. Their lives were dominated by the 'hwyl'. Welsh preaching in the past was more than doctrine or rhetoric – it was poetry. Unprogressive? Perhaps. Narrow? Yes. Bigoted? Without a doubt. But there was something in it which lifted the listeners, which poured from the mouth of the preacher in a white heat of emotion and left his spirit chastened from the grossness of earthly delights. It swept over the congregation and left their souls naked in the presence of *something* which they could not understand, but they knew with all the certainty of faith what was great andnoble and true. And it is that glorious uplift which I believe is the basic underlying quality of all true religions.[4]

Balliol College, Oxford 1934–6

Pennar now set his sights on Oxford and obtained a reference from Dr Olive Wheeler,[5] Cardiff's Professor of Education, in which she praised his dissertation: "This work showed that he had read widely and with insight, that he had unusual powers of sustained and ordered thought, and both in literary style and intellectual ability he was well above the average."[6] She spoke of this student as one who, given the opportunity, could make a significant contribution to the world of learning. Despite this glowing reference, thinking of Oxford was not easy for Pennar. His father had suffered two major accidents in the mine in 1926 and 1930 which had scarred him psychologically as well as physically. His fear of returning underground paralysed him. For all this he received as compensation the sum of two shillings and three pence (about 21 pence). At times a sense of guilt weighed heavily on Pennar as he thought of the tremendous sacrifices his parents had made so that he could receive an education far beyond what they and their daughters had had. This was accompanied by a regular questioning as to whether he should get a job. The quandary was solved by the arrival on their doorstop of Mrs Fitzgerald. "One day a strange lady came to our poor house, dressed in black clothes and with a veil hiding her face. She said in English, which was strangely refined, that she was anxious to give financial aid to a poor boy who deserved it."[7] This newly widowed lady had inherited both her husband's money and his desire to help the academic aspirations of poor boys. The fact that south Wales valleys at that time were among the most depressed areas in Britain brought Mrs Fitzgerald to Mountain Ash, where she enquired of the local doctor whether there was a local candidate for her sponsorship and was directed at once to 11 Duffryn Street. Pennar records the visit: "She looked inquisitively at me like someone forming an opinion about me. She showed little interest in my mother's presence and when my father appeared he received no greeting from the visitor. Her interest was solely in me. Suddenly she removed her veil. Hers was a pale, dignified face, with neither frown nor smile. I never saw her face again after that visit. Before leaving the house Mrs Fitzgerald handed me a pound note. I looked at it in amazement. My father had to risk his life and lose sweat for half a week to receive almost that much pay. After bidding farewell to the lady, we stared at each other in wonder."[8] Within two weeks, a parcel of books arrived from his sponsor, including a life of Jesus, which was to play a significant role in his life. Mrs Fitzgerald's support was sufficient to send him first to Oxford University and then to Yale University in the United States. From time to time he received postcards from her from various Swiss cities as well as her Alpine chalet. Pennar learned little about her apart from the fact that she was wealthy, bereaved and anxious to support a poor boy. This strange relationship and her sponsorship ended abruptly in 1939 when he registered as a conscientious objector at the outbreak of the Second World War.

Pennar arrived at Balliol, 'the College of the intellectual elite',[9] on 12 October 1934. He described his rooms in college to his mother who responded, "I hope that you are comfortable and happy, dear, and I am glad that you have a fire, also a bathroom at last" – unheard of luxury for most of the south Wales valleys people of the 1930s. At Balliol he made friends with several Indians who later became prominent in the life of their country, as well as English and Scottish students from aristocratic and wealthy families. At the invitation of his old friend, J Gwyn Griffiths, he joined the Dafydd ap Gwilym Society, the university's prestigious gathering of Welsh students. Among these were a number who would later play an important part in the nation's life; amongst them, Gwynfor Evans held a particular significance.[10] However, Pennar remained a quiet and shy individual, feeling rather uncomfortable in the company of so many loud and privileged young men, and it was its academic gifts that Balliol bestowed upon him. At the end of his two years, his thesis on 'John Bale and his Dramatic Works' gained him the outstanding praise

29

of his examiner C S Lewis, and Oxford University's degree of B.Litt. Part of his work was published in the *Transactions of the Oxford Literary Society* in 1939 with the title, 'A Bibliography of John Bale'. The new Bachelor of Letters was given further academic recognition with the award of a Commonwealth Fund Fellowship to study in any university in the world. He chose Yale.

4

The Time of his Life
1936–8

PENNAR ARRIVED AT Yale in Connecticut at the end of the summer of 1936, and registered as a student in the university's graduate school, becoming a member of Branford College. He soon came to enjoy and appreciate his new situation. "I enjoyed my time at Yale, from 1936 to 1938. I was a Commonwealth Fund Fellow, and that meant a comfortable income, such as I had never enjoyed before and shall never enjoy again."[1] This Welshman took to Yale in a way that he never did to Oxford, living in a style beyond his parents' imagining and enjoying luxuries far exceeding their dreams. He became a keen supporter of the university (American) football team and broadened his cultural interests to encompass music and the visual arts. He attended opera at the New York Metropolitan as well as the weekly classical concerts at Yale's Woolsey Hall. He was in his element. He and a new friend, Ted Taylor, made a 3,300-mile car journey across the States in the summer of 1937, taking in New Jersey, Pennsylvania, Maryland, Virginia, Kentucky and Tennessee, before heading west to New Mexico and then California. This is described by him in two unpublished works, a description of the journey and a detailed diary. He describes "this magnificent expanse of country... with bewildering intimations of vast wealth and terrifying barrenness and grotesque extravagance and supremely intimate beauty". This Welshman was particularly interested

31

in America's ethnic minorities, Afro-Americans, Mexicans (who vividly reminded him of "the industrial proletariat of south Wales") and Native Americans. A month after leaving Yale, the duo arrived at Santa Fe, New Mexico. He met the writer, Haniel Long, and a friendship developed which lasted until Long's death in 1956.[2] In later years, J Gwyn Griffiths wrote that, "During the confessional sessions of the Cadwgan circle Pennar used to speak of a ceremonial espousal with the 'Grey Lizard', an Indian girl from Mexico." In the 1950s Pennar himself wrote that "there are sexual experiences in the story of each of us of which we cannot speak to our closest friends".[3] These references to his 'sexual experiences' in America were never truly explained, although some of his poems refer to close friendships which he had with a number of women at Yale.

After a memorably happy time at Santa Fe, the friends moved on to California, where Pennar was appalled by Los Angeles, "the Babylon of Ballyhoo". He loved San Francisco but it was the wide open spaces that really captivated him, with all the glories of nature. Of Yosemite and Yellowstone he wrote, "I had seen it all before in romantic poetry". They then headed north as far as Seattle and turned east again through Wyoming and Montana towards Chicago ("... more primitive than Babylon. Here was Babel, stricken with a confusion of appetites and itches; competition roved in murderous frenzy everywhere."), and then through Detroit, Buffalo and Syracuse, skirting the Great Lakes. The civilization he saw seemed like "Dwarfdom threatening the whole world like a horrid cloud of locusts". All the time he and his mother shared a regular correspondence; he describing his journeys and experiences and she giving news of home, family and chapel, but with some references to outside events, such as the Spanish Civil War, Edward VIII and Mrs Simpson, and the burning of the Llŷn Bombing School at Penyberth.[4] When referring to the financial hardships of the family and their neighbours she added, "but we poor people could do with a bit more joy in our lives".[5] More than the wonder of the land and the romantic experiences he underwent, it was the meeting of great minds and the clash of intellectual debate that was Yale's greatest gift to the young Welshman. His two closest friends were Augustus Baer (1917–65), who became a Benedictine monk, teaching English at a school attached to his monastery, and Clem Linnenberg (born 1912), an economist who had a distinguished career in the U.S. civil service and who kept in close touch with Pennar for the next fifty years.

His diaries from that period in college were quite scathing of some of his fellow students. He was critical of the social pretensions and snobbery of some of the Yale graduates that he mixed with. This may well have been associated with the guilt that he felt at having himself moved far from his working-class upbringing. At the same time, it is abundantly clear that he enjoyed his time in the United States immensely. It was in his unpublished diary at this time that he gave the fullest account of his childhood at Mountain Ash:

> I recalled the poverty of my childhood and youth today – with a shock. I remember periods when none of us saw an egg for months and lived on bread and butter and tea for days. I remember four children sharing two eggs between us. I remember my mother crying very quietly but helplessly, broken under the strain of the slow, merciless terror – Friday after Friday as she fingered the money Dad had brought home – eight shillings or less, perhaps to keep us on or pay 'clubs' after paying the rent. I remember the occasions on which my father went out for long walks – to be absent for meals when there was not enough food for us. I remember that time when mother wept for gratitude and love when Mrs Griffiths sent her a parcel of food hoping she would not be 'offended'... Dad was in hospital with that first horrible accident.[6]

Despite the whirl which was his social life Pennar continued to excel academically. In the 1938 examination necessary before beginning on his Ph.D., Pennar passed "with honors". His examiner, G H Nettleton, commented that "Restoration drama is well served and firmly evaluated". He had a similar success in his oral examination. His mammoth thesis of nine hundred pages in two volumes, at last completed in 1943, received the title, 'The Comedies of George Chapman (1559–1634) in relation to his Life and Times'. At the same time, the young Welshman was writing poetry in both English and Welsh.

5

Cardiff and Oxford Revisited

University College, Cardiff 1938–40

EVENTUALLY HIS WONDERFUL time at Yale came to an end but his place in academia was retained through the awarding of a University of Wales Fellowship at Cardiff, enabling him to continue studying until 1940. He applied for posts at several universities in England and Northern Ireland but he longed for a post in one of the English departments of the federal University of Wales.

All this while, Pennar's inner spiritual turmoil continued as he battled between atheism, agnosticism and faith. He had written in 1938: "I rejected the necessity for any means of grace. I rejected the whole notion of something higher than myself which it was necessary for me to contact. I knew nothing higher than myself. I was the most complete incarnation of God that I knew, and so I was not merely un-Christian but anti-Christian."[1] The end of 1939 saw a remarkable change as he committed himself firmly to the Christian faith. According to Gwynfor Evans, this change was linked to the crisis for Wales and the world on the eve of World War II;[2] though Professor Densil Morgan in his biography of Pennar insists that the change is surrounded by mystery and describes Pennar's own comment as 'cryptic': "Turning from agnosticism... God is here overcoming my negativity and giving meaning to life."[3] It seems clear that, despite his 'living it up' in America and all his debating with his Yale friends, Pennar was all the time battling with something basic inside himself. While something major undoubtedly happened, little is known of the details. He writes in 'Clawr Coch': "As I meditated in this way I had a glimpse of the love which never falls away... Gradually there grew in my heart and conscience the conviction that the Christ who was crucified by soldiers was the true Saviour of the world." "From this time forward", writes Densil Morgan, "the Christ of the New Testament and especially of the Synoptic Gospels became both the foundation and the key to his faith." Pennar wrote to Clem Linnenberg: "When I came out to the United States in 1936 I was an agnostic, a pagan and a cynic. Since my return from America in 1938... I have given my life to the work of the Christian ministry." By the summer of 1939 the Yale alumnus had been through a conversion experience, seen by his biographer as being "not of an evangelical variety but rather one which saw everything as fulfilling its purpose in God, with Jesus of Nazareth". Pennar himself told Welsh-language poet and friend, Alun Llywelyn-Williams,[4] in 1940 that, "I am a keen and sincere Christian and resolute according to my own interpretation".[5]

September 1939 saw two events which were to have a great influence on the boy from Mountain Ash. The first was the outbreak of war on 3 September. The other was the marriage of his close friend, J Gwyn Griffiths, to the German-Jewish Egyptologist refugee, Dr Käthe (Kate) Bosse,[6] whom he met at Oxford. They set up home at a house called Cadwgan in the shadow of Moel Cadwgan, the mountain separating the two Rhondda valleys at this point. Gwyn had been appointed junior History teacher at the Rhondda County Boys' School in Porth, where he himself had been a pupil, and where he taught the author in his first year. No sooner were they settled than their home became the meeting place of a group of authors and poets who were to make a significant contribution to Welsh literature in the twentieth century. It was in *Cylch Cadwgan* (the Cadwgan Circle) that this young thinker found inspiration and encouragement such as he had never experienced at Cardiff, Oxford or Yale, despite the happy memories and lasting friendships made at the latter. In addition to Gwyn, the members included his brothers, Dafydd (D R Griffiths,[7] later lecturer in New Testament Studies at Cardiff Baptist College), and Gwilym, who was training to be a teacher; he became head of several secondary schools in north Wales. Later they were joined by Rhondda Baptist minister, Rhydwen Williams,[8] the musician brothers John[9] and Arwel Hughes,[10] and the 'baby' of the group, Gareth Alban Davies,[11] son of the Rev. T Alban Davies, Welsh Independent minister at Tonpentre. *Cylch Cadwgan* was a Christian radical group, centred on pacifism and Welsh nationalism and with a polymathic interest in literature and the arts. It was at this time that Pennar made a momentous decision: "The war which brought me to a definite and unpopular political commitment, also led me to give myself to Welsh, rather than English writing and, somewhat to my own amazement and the consternation of friends on both sides of the language fence, to the quaint work of a 'respected' among the unspeakable chapel people."[12] Whether he was correct in his decision to write only in Welsh is something on which his admirers are divided. Clearly his concern was to support a minority language under serious threat of extinction, and this won him many admirers; at the same time, some people feel that it was a tragedy that he abandoned his very rich written English, which could have been used to great effect to present the claims and needs of Wales as well as the Gospel itself.

Pennar's decision to abandon any thought of teaching English Literature at a university in favour of seeking ordination caused consternation in many quarters, not least among his family and his group of intimate friends in *Cylch Cadwgan*. Pennar had sacrificed much to follow his academic interests and now he was about to throw them aside to follow a calling which earned considerably less, both in cash and in social status. His friend from his Oxford days, May Davies, was among the first to respond: "Your card today simply stunned me – put me completely out of action", whilst Alun Llywelyn-Williams wrote, "I must admit that the content of your last letter came as quite a shock. I can't imagine you as a preacher and I truly believe that the ministry will damage your muse... Never sacrifice your single-mindedness nor your literary freedom on the altar of a respectable career in the ministry. Wales has enough poet-preachers but there is only one Davies Aberpennar."[13] Even committed Welsh Congregationalist, Gwynfor Evans, expressed shock: "My first reaction was one of amazement, surprise at your courage... Despite the complaints of elderly spinsters and the malice of embittered deacons, I can only rejoice that Nonconformity has gained such a brilliant talent. If a man feels that he *must* enter it, then there is no more splendid calling."[14]

What, perhaps, caused at least as much consternation was his decision to abandon writing in the English Language, in which he was outstandingly gifted, in order to confine himself to writing in Welsh. Until now he had moved in what were then known as 'Anglo-Welsh' circles, being acquainted with the Swansea set of Dylan Thomas and Vernon Watkins and, particularly, with Keidrych Rhys.[15] He was still known as Bill Davies or W T Davies, sometimes as Davies Aberpennar; it was only later he adopted Pennar originally as a pen name: "I took the name 'Pennar' to save myself from the foreign and dull ordinariness of my English name, my three names lacking in charm. I chose 'Pennar' because the riverlet 'Pennar' flowed down to the river Cynon less than a furlong from my birthplace."

Pennar's fellowship at Cardiff ended in June 1940. Nothing had come of his attempts to secure academic appointments and so he applied for a post in the West Sussex Education

Office, headed by Evan Davis, former Director of Education for Pembrokeshire, whose interest in his young compatriot had been roused by Mrs Fitzgerald, his sponsor. Pennar's registering as a conscientious objector lost him this job as well as her sponsorship.

Mansfield College, Oxford 1941–3

He returned home to Mountain Ash, where, to the great delight of the folk at Providence, he informed his minister, the Rev. Idris Evans, of his desire to train for the ministry. With every assistance from Idris Evans, he went through the normal Congregational channels to become an ordinand and was accepted at Mansfield College, Oxford, for training. The delight of the Providence minister and congregation was not echoed by his inner group of friends in *Cylch Cadwgan* as is revealed by fellow member and fellow minister, Rhydwen Williams, in his novel *Adar y Gwanwyn* (1972). This is based on five of the circle, though it is with four of them that the novel is particularly concerned – Rhydwen (Iwan Owen), Pennar (John Rhymni Morgan), and Gwyn and Käthe Griffiths (Garmon and Elsa Elis). The novel bears out the fact that these friends were completely shocked by the news.[16] (See Appendix III)

In later years Pennar admitted to a sense of guilt at not entering a Welsh college, but Oxford and its Bodleian Library held great appeal for one still working on his doctoral thesis. Under its principal, Nathaniel Micklem,[17] Mansfield at that time was a centre both of neo-orthodoxy[18] and 'high' Congregationalism. But Pennar did not feel drawn by either of these tendencies. Instead he drew closer to the old-fashioned liberal thinker, C J Cadoux,[19] a pacifist and opponent of creeds. Despite this, the new student soon won the regard and respect of his principal. Professor R Tudur Jones records a conversation with Nathaniel Micklem in 1946 in which the latter stated that "Bill Davies was the quickest learner ever to go through my hands".[20] As 'Davies Aberpennar' he continued

writing in Welsh, with eighteen contributions appearing in
Cylch Cadwgan's journal between August 1939 and August
1940. He took a prominent part too in the Dafydd ap Gwilym
Society. And it was here that he met Rosemarie Wolff.

6

Rosemarie

ROSEMARIE WAS BORN on 13 May 1917 in the town of Mücheln, in the Saalekreis district of Saxony-Anhalt, the daughter of family doctor Paul Walter Wolff and Helena Louise (née Schaper). The family moved from Mücheln to Detmold and then to Berlin. Rosemarie was the elder of two daughters. Her sister Brigitte died in 1996, a few months before Pennar.

Her mother, Helena, was one of eight children and, like Rosemarie, lived to the age of 92. One of her brothers, Edzard Schaper (1908–84) was a well-known German author, whose work has received international acclaim. Rosemarie's father was of Jewish extraction, which can be traced back to Danzig (Gdansk), where his mother, Clara Freymuth, was born.

Despite Rosemarie's success in her Abitur examinations (similar to A Level) in Berlin, there was little hope of further study in Nazi Germany. So her parents arranged for her to come to Britain in 1938. She was welcomed by fellow German refugees, Dr Leo Liepmann and his wife Elizabeth. Leo was also related to the Freymuth family and through him the family became acquainted with Jürgen Freymuth, who had studied at Oxford University after the war, before becoming a successful judge in the Berlin courts

Rosemarie acted on the advice of her former headmistress and obtained a Society of Friends sponsorship to work as a nurse, first in Middlesborough and then at the John Radcliffe Hospital in Oxford, where a nurse Wolff and a nurse Fox worked in the same ward, a fact which was a source of great humour. Rosemarie and Merthyr Crochet-Fox developed a long-standing friendship. At Oxford she had also come to know Käthe Bosse, a graduate member of Somerville College, who was working at the Ashmolean whose common room was being shared by John Radcliffe nurses at this time. The two had much in common: both fathers were doctors of Jewish ancestry and both families were Lutheran. As the war reached its darkest hour for Britain, Mansfield College became a centre for German refugees, among whom was Lutheran pastor Dr Hans Herbert Kramm.[1] He was a friend of Dietrich Bonhoeffer, a prominent member of the Confessing Church, who began leading German services at Mansfield for his compatriots. In May 1939, Käthe married Pennar's friend from his undergraduate days at Cardiff, John Gwyn Griffiths, and it was they who introduced the German nurse to the Welsh ordinand at Mansfield College. Pennar records in 'Clawr Coch' how "at first sight I was enchanted by this beautiful refugee and the door to the nurses' home in north Oxford opened to me". Pennar later proposed by telegram, "Would you consider marrying an unorthodox, penniless Welsh poet?" They were married at Mansfield College Chapel on 26 June 1943, with Herbert Kramm officiating at the Lutheran service, assisted by John Marsh, later principal at Mansfield, and with Eric Routley[2] as best man. Rosemarie's influence led Pennar to learn German and, like her friend Käthe, she learned Welsh quickly. Therefore a second German woman was drawn into the Welsh circles at Oxford, where she met several of Pennar's friends, including Gwynfor Evans, and later *Cylch Cadwgan* at the Griffiths' home in Pentre, Rhondda.

The young German refugee brought few worldly goods with her from Germany, but one proved to be of exceptional value – an Erika typewriter. It was on this machine, possessing a range of accents lacking on British machines, that Pennar typed whilst on honeymoon in Cornwall. Indeed, for the next 40 years, it was on this typewriter that Pennar composed most of his literary and academic works, until finally succumbing to an electric model. Rosemarie often told her family jokingly that he had married her for her Erika, adding that he spent much of their honeymoon typing up a college dissertation. Rosemarie, as the character of Turbida in his confessional diary *Cudd fy Meiau* revealed, could be quite feisty. Apart from the typewriter, his bride brought with her a great culinary skill and a vast knowledge of traditional German recipes. Every celebration, religious or family, had a German flavour to it, including the decorations.

The marriage of the daughter of a German doctor to the son of a Welsh coal miner must have brought a change of world for her, especially as her husband chose to walk his own unique path. She had studied English and French at school and had scarcely mastered English when she had to learn a third language. She was welcomed into the Carmarthenshire home of Aneurin Talfan Davies and his family, and was saturated in Welshness and the Welsh language. In later years she found an interest in English Literature and was able to attend classes at University College of Wales, Swansea, and also classes in Italian.

The young Congregationalist probably did not realise when he proposed that Rosemarie had brought a wealth of religious tradition and practice to him and his ministry. Although her family was Lutheran Christian, there was a Jewish candelabrum in their home. Aunt Wilma, a nun, sent German Catholic decorations to the family each Christmas. Uncle Edzard also became a Catholic after belonging to the Greek Orthodox Church for some years. Whilst at the Radcliffe hospital, Rosemarie spent several Christmas and Easter holidays with the Quaker family of her friend Merthyr. Whereas Leo Lipmann had also become a Quaker, his wife Elizabeth belonged to the German Lutheran congregation which met at Mansfield College Chapel. The results of the coming together of Rosemarie's rich background and Pennar's worldwide links were obvious in their home and family life.

For two periods after marriage she returned to nursing at

Swansea and Llanelli. But, for most of the time, she devoted herself to caring for her husband and children, supporting him in his ministry and his campaigning for Wales and its language, and encouraging them as they sought their own ways forward in life. It is said that saints and idealists are not always easy people with whom to live nor is genteel poverty always easy to bear, but Rosemarie succeeded in doing just that, without complaint and with a smile for those who spoke to her. As Pennar gradually succumbed to Alzheimer's disease she nursed him with tenderness and love.

She continued to live in the family home with Geraint and Meirion, receiving in her turn loving care from her eldest child for more than seven years, before moving to the Hillside residential home to receive tender care from its staff during her last days. She died 8 February 2010.

Shepherd of his Flock

ALTHOUGH PENNAR HAD begun to preach in Welsh, it was obvious to him and his friends that his spoken Welsh was stiff and unnatural, so when the time came to choose a field of service, he reluctantly decided to seek am English-language pastorate. In December 1942 he received a call to the English Congregational Church at Minster Road, Cardiff, and was ordained there on 21 July 1943. Of the church's ninety members, a dozen were serving in the armed forces. Nonetheless they gave a unanimous call to this pacifist Welsh nationalist with a German wife, and the call was matched by the warmth of the welcome given to both of them. The stipend was £200 per annum with eight free Sundays on which he could conduct worship at other churches.

Ministerial duties did not necessitate turning his back on former interests. Sadly for him, Gwyn and Käthe Griffiths moved to Bala so that Gwyn could take up his new post at its county school in September 1943, but this marked the beginning of a regular correspondence. Pennar, at the request of Gwynfor Evans, wrote a pamphlet on federalism, *Ffederaliaeth*, for the Welsh Peace Society – Gwyn Griffiths praised it, describing its author as the 'Welsh Grundtvig'.[1] The pamphlet also opened a growing friendship between Pennar and Gwynfor, marked by a regular interchange of letters, in which they shared secret thoughts on the state of society and the obstacles to the establishment of a free Wales. 'Clawr Coch' contains a letter to D R Griffiths, who was by now a Baptist minister in Caerleon, in which he describes the affection shared between minister and congregation at Minster Road:

> Most of the congregation have come to express interest in my sermons and in their relationship to each other... It was possible for me in my church in Cardiff to declare completely openly that the gospel of Jesus Christ is a gospel of peace, and I received plenty of respect and sympathy... Throughout my stay the people of Minster Road were delightfully supportive.

Densil Morgan records how his pastorate was remembered with great pleasure at the Cardiff church: "His charming personality, devotional conduct of the services and thought-provoking sermons captivated all who heard him."[2] The worship he led at Minster Road revealed that though he had rejected the ruling theology at his college, its churchmanship had rubbed off on him. He introduced liturgical elements into his services, following the Christian Year, and established a prayer meeting before Sunday morning worship. More than that he was caught up in the sense of the wholeness of the Church and of its catholic nature, referring to himself as "a catholic in the Congregational tradition". The attachment of this liberal and catholic minister to the person of Christ was strong indeed as he shared his understanding of Christ and his gospel with his people. Typical is the way in which he dealt with the Resurrection: "If you truly believe in God, it is not difficult to believe in the Resurrection... Isn't it the most credible thing in the world to believe that God should preserve his own? There is nothing unusual about the Resurrection of Jesus. If you believe in God and in Christ as the Incarnation of God, you must believe in the Resurrection."[3]

The Minster Road years were particularly happy for Pennar and not only because of the response of his congregation. His proximity to Mountain Ash enabled him to pay regular visits to his parents and to his sisters. All of them took great pleasure in his academic success and supported him in his chosen field of service, and did so in spite of his pacifism (so far removed from his father's fond remembrances of his own military service), his nationalism and his strong Christian convictions. His marriage to a German girl was more difficult to accept but that problem solved itself when their first child, Andreas Meirion, was born in 1944. However, despite the happy state of his relations with both family and church, it was obvious that the young minister required a greater challenge.

Church Historian

ILLNESS AMONG THE staff at Mansfield in the summer of
1944 placed extra burdens on John Marsh, who found himself
teaching biblical subjects in addition to his own Philosophy of
Religion course. There was talk that Pennar would be invited
to be his assistant. In the event the post went to someone else
but Pennar had been shown that he was held in high regard
at Mansfield, even though his theology was far removed from
that of Nathaniel Micklem and John Marsh. There was still
the opportunity of moving to a larger Welsh-speaking church.
Although Gwynfor Evans assured Pennar that there was no need
for him to be concerned about his spoken Welsh, reminding
him that a year's constant use of the language would bring
about a huge difference, he himself had doubts. Meanwhile
he had promised to continue writing in English and several of
his poems appeared in *Modern Welsh Poetry*, edited by his old
friend Keidrich Rhys. He also wrote a number of articles under
a series of pseudonyms for Plaid Cymru's *Ap*, 'A Collection of
writings in English', which he edited. He began broadcasting
and scripting for the BBC's Welsh Home Service. On the first
occasion he spoke of his experiences at Yale. Then he debated
with Keidrych Rhys on the relationship of Welsh literature
with Anglo-Welsh writing. There followed his series of talks
on Welsh poets writing in Welsh or English. The content of the
writings and broadcasts of Davies Aberpennar, as he wished
to be known, came as a great surprise to friends from the old
days who were unaware of his conversion to both Christianity

and Welsh nationalism. Pennar's vision received its clearest expression to date when he edited a booklet entitled *The Welsh Pattern* for the Religion and Life Fellowship, an ecumenical group of young ministers, who met at Llanmadog on the Gower Peninsula. In the booklet he set out the history of Welsh religion, claiming that his fellow countrymen had taken the social content of the Gospel more seriously than anyone else: "Christianity among the early Welsh was far more than a matter of individual piety or ecclesiastical order; it was a social movement. It stood for liberty, co-operation and the common weal." Pennar felt that he was part of this heritage, which had been renewed by Nonconformity.[1]

Soon afterwards the end of the war in Europe was declared. He led his congregation in celebration and in looking forward to seeing their young people return home, adding this warning: "We must weep because such things are possible in a part of the world where Christianity has been taught for nearly two thousand years."[2] For Pennar himself, the cessation of hostilities brought sadness too with the news that Käthe Bosse's mother had died in Ravensbruck Concentration Camp, the main camp for women. Her brothers were imprisoned but then worked in a concentration camp for foreigners; their death sentence was not carried out at the end of the war. Other relatives perished in various camps, including Thersienstadt.[3] Rosemarie had no news of her family for years and lived in constant fear that they had been sent to concentration camps. Now she learned that although her mother and sister had survived, that her father had died of colitis before the outbreak of the war because Jews were refused admission to hospitals. Other members of her family had died in the camps also. Then the conflict in the Far East ended with the dropping of atomic bombs on Hiroshima and Nagasaki, raising questions for many people about what the future might bring.

However, 1946 brought its own excitement to the Minster Road manse. Early in the year there was talk of a post in the English department at Aberystwyth, where its head, Professor

Gwyn Jones, himself a noted author in English, was anxious that Pennar should submit his application. Then John Morgan Jones, principal of Coleg Bala-Bangor, the Welsh Independent seminary at Bangor, died on 6 March of that year. Professor J E Daniel, who in normal events should have expected to succeed as principal, failed to do so because of his strong commitment to the Welsh nationalist cause and because of his wife's conversion to Roman Catholicism. He resigned his post to become an inspector of schools. Thus both teaching posts at Bangor were vacant. Pennar decided to apply for the principalship and his close friend Gwynfor Evans wrote to say that he had the backing of J E Daniel. There followed a period of quite intense correspondence between Pennar and his two closest friends. On the matter of Bala-Bangor, Gwynfor Evans commented in a letter dated 18 January 1946, "I do not know the method of appointing, but I fear that the appointment will be in the hands of some people who have not had the opportunity to know you". Another letter followed on 24 February, following a month of denominational gossip and rumours: "Jack Daniel eagerly supports your candidacy for the principalship, but some of the old hands feel that someone 'safe' is needed to shepherd the college carefully for a period of years, and restore its relationship with the churches. Under John Morgan Jones it distanced itself from them and that was before the modernism of Thomas Rees led it into deep waters. The feeling is that a minister is needed... The Rev. R J Jones, Cardiff, is a favourite... I do not know how strong a chance you have in the face of all of this, but I fear that the above reasoning could carry the day."

J Gwyn Griffiths, in a letter dated 23 February, foresaw difficulties with regard to Bala-Bangor, especially in view of Pennar's youth. Yet, without discouraging his application but, at the same time, setting out a strong case for the English post at Aberystwyth, he remarked: "It is possible that your youth will be against your candidacy for the principal's job. It is doubtful whether the Independents would be ready to entrust such a responsible and important post to someone so young... but I can easily imagine that you could be accepted by them as a professor – becoming principal later on... At Aber, and in the English Department, there would be a new opportunity to discuss English literature from the point of view of the Gospel, to cause a powerful explosion under 'the mighty concrete of Philistia'."

The views of his wife Käthe, were added: "Käthe, as you might expect, strongly favours Aber. She says that it would save your soul." Next day, 24 February, Gwynfor Evans wrote again: "I have considered the matter of Aberystwyth and come to the conclusion that the argument in favour of trying for the post is one from which there is no retreat; if the choice is between going there and remaining in your present church. Though I should like to see you at Bala-Bangor, there is the possibility of fulfilling a great work for the cause of Christ in such a post [i.e. at Aberystwyth]. The influence of your energetic, militant Christianity would be felt throughout the College and the University... Your leadership could cause the colleges to become less pagan than they are now."

Pennar applied for the Bangor principalship in March 1946, with the publicly expressed support of J E Daniel, Nathaniel Micklem and John Marsh. The college council, elected by subscribers, chose Gwilym Bowyer, conveniently placed as minister of Ebenezer Welsh Independent Church at Bangor and better known on the denomination's preaching circuit than in academic circles. Pennar plucked the second string in his bow, successfully applying on 12 April for the Aberystwyth lectureship. His success troubled him for it meant leaving Cardiff, where he was in easy reach of his parents and congregation, turning his back on the ministry and all that involved, and causing disappointment to many people who saw him as one who could bring new hope to a steadily weakening Nonconformity. At the same time, he was pleased, telling Gwyn Jones, his new professor, that "I was jubilant over the Aberystwyth appointment".

But this was not to be. He was informed on 16 April that the Bala-Bangor college council had decided, without first approaching Pennar, to offer him the post of Professor of Church History, at the college, which was part of the university's Faculty of Theology. He chose Bangor for half the salary he would have received at Aberystwyth. The induction service for the two new colleagues was held at a Bangor church under the presidency of Dr H Elvet Lewis.[4] Pennar now found himself in a Welsh-speaking scholarly community. He was delighted with his new post. But, this was followed by a return to Mountain Ash early in 1947 for his father's funeral.

Mansfield College celebrated its fiftieth anniversary in that year and the college authorities invited the young Cardiff minister to write its history. The booklet *Mansfield College, Oxford: Its History, Aims and Achievements* appeared in 1947. A reviewer in the college magazine said of it that "It is a very interesting and readable document and it contains an extraordinary amount of information considering its size". Nathaniel Micklem was quite ecstatic: "This really is a first-class piece of work, and I am much more than happy to think that your first publication as a Professor of Church History should be the story of Mansfield." The summer of 1947 saw the death of C J Cadoux and therefore a vacant chair of Church History at Mansfield. Three ministers were invited to apply for the post: Pennar's friend Geoffrey Nuttall, Aubrey Vine and Pennar were to be interviewed for the post. To the great disappointment of the Mansfield principal, Pennar did not turn up: "Pennar Davies declined the invitation on the grounds that his vocation lay in Wales."[5]

Pennar soon settled into his work at Bangor, gaining the praise of colleagues and students alike. Among the latter were many young cultured nationalist Welshmen, who were later to have an important role in Wales and its churches. They included D Alun Lloyd,[6] M Islwyn Lake[7] and F M Jones;[8] all three shared his Christian nationalism and pacifism. Pennar preached every Sunday in the chapels of Gwynedd and held a very lively Welsh literature class in a nearby village. All this time, his love of Wales grew and developed, and he saw it as being linked to his Christian conversion. During this period he developed his vision of the nation as one of God's vessels, with special reference to Pennar's own people:

> The Welsh character is incurably religious; peculiarly prone to worship, sensitive to the evocations of the noble and the beautiful... Cymru has always been sensitive to the presence and purpose of the unseen but living God. And with this goes a regard for the personal dignity and social need of man, a passion for healthy freedom, a readiness to rebel against tyrannies and uniformities, a respect for spiritual power and moral integrity as against worldly authority and brute force, and on the other hand a deep sense of obligation to one's kith and kin, to the family, the clan, the nation, to humanity, to the ideal society.[9]

Pennar found himself increasingly busy as a father, litterateur, college professor and preacher. Something had to go. In a letter to Nathaniel Micklem on the question of his B.D., he wrote, "I say all this to show that the unfinished B.D. is not a sign of laziness but of a tendency to undertake more than I can cope with."[10] Certainly his students at Brecon in the 1950s would agree, especially as the tendency seemed to grow. In addition to church history, Pennar was interested in creative writing and literary criticism (in both English and Welsh), New Testament studies and practical politics. To supplement his meagre income in Brecon, which began to fall behind even the stipends of ministers in pastorates, he also undertook the marking of school certificate examination papers and was often seen at this task on a bus to and from preaching engagements. His students at Brecon later saw in this a tendency to dilettantism. As Densil Morgan stressed in Pennar's biography, his professor at Mansfield, Nathaniel Micklem had warned him not to divide his interests too much, but partly driven by financial necessity and partly because he was, in the words of Professor Dewi Eirug Davies, something of a 'polymath', he didn't heed the warning.

9

Pastor Pastorum

LIFE WAS SOON to change again for the Davies family. Nathaniel Micklem made contact with Pennar after attending a meeting at the Congregational Memorial College, Brecon, where he heard that the committee wished Pennar to become Professor of Church History, replacing Isaac Thomas, who was moving over to teach New Testament studies, following the death of Professor Joseph Jones.[1] "You will have noticed that they have shifted their Church History man to the NT in order to get you. That means a very great deal... I hope that you will feel it as a call. I think it should be an immense opportunity to serve the church in Wales."[2]

The 'shift' noted by Mansfield's principal was not as easy as he made it sound. There is no hint here as to Isaac Thomas' feelings on the subject. These are revealed in the Rev. Ieuan Davies' fine new biography of Isaac Thomas, *Gwerthfawrogiad o Fywyd a Gwaith Dr Isaac Thomas, 1911–2004,*[3] [An appreciation of the life and work of Dr Isaac Thomas, 1911–2004] where he quotes from Thomas' tribute to W D Davies[4] in the Welsh Independents' weekly *Y Tyst* in August 2001. He describes Davies as one of "... the leading scholars of the twentieth century" adding that "it was inevitable in view of the success of *Paul and Rabbinic Judaism* [a work which gained Davies a D.D. from the University of Wales] ... would be encouraged to seek the services of W D. He was appointed Professor of New Testament at the United College, Bradford, but his heartfelt desire was to return to Wales, and when the Professor of New

Testament at Memorial College, Dr Joseph Jones, died, he believed that his opportunity had come. But that was not the judgment of the committees of Memorial College, Brecon, and Bala-Bangor. Despite his peerless qualifications he was not appointed." Ieuan Davies adds: "The disappointment and pain felt by W D also caused deep disappointed and hurt to his true friend."

Two years later the same college committee appointed Pennar as principal. Ieuan Davies asks, "How, one wonders, did Isaac Thomas feel two years later? It was not he, who had served the college in various ways with brilliance and thoroughness for nine years, who was chosen to be the new principal there in 1952 , but Pennar Davies, who served there as professor for just two years. But was it on the understanding that he would be promoted to the principalship that Pennar agreed to leave Bala-Bangor in 1950?"[5] There would be no record of the discussions that took place prior to Pennar's original appointment to Brecon, and one guess is as good as another, but the references to the committees of both colleges are worthy of note. Was it possible that Bala-Bangor saw a possible successor to Pennar standing in the wings, in the person of Aberystwyth minister, R Tudur Jones whereas there was no one within Wales to replace Joseph Jones, apart from Brecon's Professor of Church History, who was qualified in Greek. Both Tudur Jones and Pennar would have been acceptable as good Welshmen and good Welsh Independents, whereas W D Davies had been ordained into the English Congregational ministry in England and had worked only in that country. Who knows?

In the event, Isaac Thomas was compelled to change roles in order to make room for Pennar and this would have involved a great deal of extra work for him in preparing to teach a new subject. He might well have assumed that, in the course of time, he would become principal but again his claims were rejected in favour of the comparative newcomer. There are three observations which come immediately to mind. First, it was the committees and not Pennar Davies who were responsible for this situation. Secondly, the fact that these two men became close friends says much about the character of each of them: Isaac appears to have accepted the situation with remarkably good grace; there must have been something very special in the personality of the man from Bala-Bangor to enable this special relationship to develop as it did. Thirdly, it was perhaps providential that Isaac was driven back to his New Testament studies, for it was in these that he gave such outstanding service to Christianity in Wales and it is for these that he will be remembered.

This was the beginning of a new period in Wales as elsewhere, with the standard of living, so low in the 1920s and '30s, just beginning to rise. A sense of peace was spreading. But the revival was economic, rather than cultural and spiritual. The Welsh language, Welsh identity and Welsh Nonconformity all faced a great threat. From now on Pennar was to play a leading role in the story of Welsh, mainly Welsh-speaking, Christianity. He moved from Bangor's Welshness to the Anglicised cathedral city, county and market town of Brecon, with its barracks and army camp. Professor D J Davies summed up thus: "The important day in Brecon is when the regiment marches to the cathedral with fixed bayonets... Many fervent Nonconformists quickly become Anglicans on moving here." Professor Emeritus John Evans, who had lived in Brecon since 1894, when asked by students in 1954 for his memories of the 1904 Revival, replied, "I don't know much about the Revival. I was in Brecon at the time. Brecon people like their religion to be respectable. They want to go to heaven in a sedate way."[6]

It was to a house attached to the college that the Davies family moved. Pennar's practical theology and ideas about religion had already involved him in social and political action in north Wales. The move to Brecon did little to curb his commitment, and he returned to Gwynedd in August 1951 for the first of a number of peaceful protests against the plan to establish yet another military base in Wales, this time at Trawsfynydd. It is said that the county's police Chief Constable, Colonel Jones-

Williams,[7] a Welsh Independent deacon, came with his men to remove the 'hotheads' and was nonplussed when first he met Dr R Tudur Jones[8] sitting on the road, then Dr Pennar Davies a short distance away. One need not wonder at how Pennar's new neighbours reacted to seeing him sitting on a Merioneth road, surrounded by other protesters and policemen. As he plunged into his new duties, he found himself attending conferences, writing poetry and prose, with a host of other interests to be actively pursued, now as before.

Then, in 1952, he was appointed college principal to succeed J D Vernon Lewis, who remained on the staff as Professor of the Old Testament.[9] The college had a senate of four professors. Isaac Thomas (New Testament) and Pennar had great teaching skills, which endeared them to their students, the former with respect, the latter with love and affection as well. D J Davies (Christian Doctrine and Philosophy of Religion) was no academic but a kindly man, who immersed himself in the cultural life of the county.[10] Many of his illustrative anecdotes, which invariably began with the phrase "When I was in the ministry in Neath", proved useful to at least some of his students in later years. Vernon Lewis was by the mid-1950s an old man, erratic in his thoughts and teachings, prone to favour some and bully those who would not stand up to him, and felt by the students, rightly or wrongly, to be unhappy to have surrendered the principal's post to Pennar. The college had not been tainted by modern ideas of ministerial training and community life. Pennar and D J Davies occupied houses attached to the college; the others lived a short distance away.

This was a particularly difficult time for the college. There was a great shortage of candidates, especially for the Welsh-language ministry, and the staff made a point of seeking out possible candidates so as to get hold of them before some other seminary did, alongside which came the danger of lowering entrance standards in order to secure adequate numbers. The Memorial College depended on the gifts of individual church members, a practice which had not changed in decades. Each student was given a collecting list of churches at which to preach. How the collecting actually took place varied from church to church, and ranged from a simple appeal, to read aloud the previous year's donors and their generous shillings or half crowns, to having to call at the supporters' houses and coax their support for another year. The burden fell most heavily on the small group of Welsh speakers, for most support came from the Welsh Independent churches. There were two lists – one for the college year, when Sunday visits were arranged to churches in south Wales, the other involving a month or so in north Wales in the summer, moving from church to church and house to house each day. Students received a small commission, of great value to those who received no grants. The college had been built when it was easy to get servants to live and work in underground quarters. Only staff and guests were allowed to use the magnificent staircase, except when students carried their luggage in and out at the beginning and end of each term; otherwise they used a narrow, winding staircase at the end of a corridor, probably intended for Victorian servants. There were two indoor toilets for night use only; during the day, students used an outside convenience, whatever the weather, just as the oldest professor would had done when a student fifty years earlier.

Seven new students, three of whom were Welsh-speaking, were welcomed to Coleg Coffa (Memorial College) Brecon by all four members of the senate in October 1953. They included two graduates and an army sergeant-major, whilst most of the others had some sort of work experience. They were thus instructed: "You will get up at 7 a.m. and have breakfast at 8 a.m. You will attend lectures between 9 a.m. and 1 p.m. After lunch you will go out and get some exercise. On Tuesday to Friday, sacred hours last from 5.30 p.m. to 7 a.m., when you may not leave the building. Sacred hours end at noon on Saturday and re-commence at 6 a.m. on Monday, to give you time to fulfil your preaching engagements." I forget who issued these instructions but it was not the principal (incidentally the only member of the senate not to have been a Brecon student himself). The only social contact with the three lecturers was when each took his week's duty to have lunch with the students. Only Pennar joined the students in morning prayers, shared a sermon class, or invited students into his home and showed personal interest in each of them. The principal also added extra classes to the curriculum. There were courses in Welsh on the history of Welsh Nonconformity and Welsh Hymnody. The students requested that he speak to them about human sexuality, with special reference to the then taboo subject of homosexuality. He did so willingly and led them into a world much of which was new to most of them. When, some years later, the Mens' Fellowship at Wern Congregational Church, Aberavon, asked its minister to find someone to explain the changes in the law regarding homosexuality, I contacted Pennar and he accepted the invitation immediately. The assembled gathering had little idea beforehand of what was going to happen: the guest speaker spoke at length, using the legal terms involved and explaining them. He was heard in deep silence, which continued when he had finished. At last, one of the members, a foreman on the coal exporting dock said, "I have heard words used here in chapel tonight which I did not like hearing at the docks". In fairness, the speaker had only done what they had requested; it was not his fault that it was too much for them.

The magnificent college building was in a deplorable condition – in 1953 the students took it on themselves to decorate their rooms at their own expense, the college council deciding later to reimburse them. (When I took a coach load of church members on a tour of the college in 1957 we were shown around the building by the principal, who was anxious to point out the oil portraits of former principals on the dining room wall; it was left to me to make sure that they saw the cracks in the walls. The purpose of the visit had been to encourage financial support for the college.) The matron retired in 1954

59

and a couple, who had left the service of the college so that the wife to become the cook to the Lord Mayor of Liverpool, returned to Memorial College for a year, when the students ate like lords, to the consternation of the college treasurer.

10

Tribulation and Trust

A NEW COUPLE came to the college in 1955, with little understanding of their respective roles as caretaker and cook. The quality of meals rapidly deteriorated. One day the saintly David Bowen warned his fellow students not to eat the meat because it was bad.[1] As discontent grew, so the students met together frequently to discuss the situation. Gradually a list of complaints and requests, including some to do with the standard of some of the teaching, was presented to and rejected by the senate. The tension grew and the student body unanimously decided to strike as no one would listen to it. Unfortunately, the principal was away for several days and did not return until late on the night of Monday, 14 November. This meant that the student president could not inform him that a strike was to begin at 9 a.m. until morning prayers next day, Tuesday, 15 November. Pennar invited the students to meet the staff but they refused, saying that they needed to speak with either the executive or the house committee. Senate reaction was swift and strong, calling on the students to attend lectures next day on pain of suspension. Their negative response led to the suspension of the whole student body on Wednesday, 16 November 1955. The students crowded together into a study and talked about their personal futures if expelled. There was almost an even division between those who put their Congregationalism first and those whose primary concern was a call to the ministry. Again the students refused to meet the senate and a joint meeting of the executive and house committee took place, at which the students were allowed to state their case.

Meanwhile, the students had been shaken by the reply, in stiff legal language, of solicitor D Gethin Williams and Judge Sir George Clark Williams,[2] to a round-robin letter sent by the students to every committee member. A small committee was set up to interview (or more accurately cross-examine) each professor and by the following Sunday the strike had ended. The couple left and the Lord Mayor's cook returned. In Densil Morgan's excellent volume, Isaac Thomas appears to blame Pennar for the situation, contrasting him with Ithel Jones, Principal of Cardiff Baptist College, where there was also a strike at about the same time. (These were not the first theological college strikes in Wales. In the early years of the twentieth century there was a week-long strike at the Calvinistic Methodist College at Trefecca, when Principal Rhys refused to allow the five hundred students their traditional holiday on Ascension Day so that they could go to Llanthony Abbey to hear Father Ignatius preach. It was only the abject apology given on behalf of the student body by J H Howard that prevented the principal's resignation.[3]) In the case of Coleg Coffa it was fortunate that the story did not reach the pages of the *Western Mail*, which happened in the case of the Baptist College. In fact it was Pennar who saved the situation from getting worse but paid dearly for being the man in the middle. He was held in deep affection by his students, who were disappointed that Isaac Thomas thought that they were criticising him, which was far from true. Sadly, Isaac Thomas decided to move to a university post at Bangor, and a split developed between him and Pennar, which ended their personal friendship.

Two incidents may throw light on the relationships within the senate and between the principal and students. On the Tuesday after Easter, the start of a new term, one student said that he had acted as best man for another student on the previous day. They all laughed at this perpetual joker. Then the groom arrived, flashing his wedding ring around. There was general excitement and no one thought that there might be archaic college rules on the matter of students getting married and needing permission to do so. At 9 a.m. on the following day, the students were informed that all lectures were cancelled and a meeting of the senate was held in the library and lasted until 12.50 p.m. It seemed that two professors demanded the immediate expulsion of the malefactor, and the other two, Isaac Thomas and Pennar, sought a more understanding approach. After a long stalemate Vernon Lewis turned to Pennar, reminding him that the principal had a casting vote. The student was thus saved. Meanwhile the students had gathered outside waiting for lunch and were by now filled with apprehension. The library door opened and Pennar, with a weary and troubled expression asked: "Where is Mr X?" The absence of the usual Christian name troubled the students even more. When the newlywed stood before him, Pennar said, "Mr X, I am instructed by the senate to severely reprimand you." Then, he added with a smile, "Don't you dare do this again!" Principal and students enjoyed their lunch together even more than usual.

Then, during one lecture, Pennar told of his great concern that he had not been baptised. He had decided on ecumenical grounds that he should be baptised: "I was going to ask one of you to do it but when a bishop said recently that it was essential, I changed my mind." Student feelings were summed up one morning when Pennar entered the lecture room, and student Lionel Walker, whose American wife was allowed to live in the town, called out, "Before you start, Dr Pennar, we all want you to know that we think you're a swell guy".

It is significant that the students wished to have their photograph taken with their principal when peace returned to the college. The students noted that, as the photograph was being taken, the other three professors walked past together, something never seen before. The student body felt, rightly or wrongly, that only Pennar Davies had shown any sympathy or understanding of the students' situation which led to the strike. Probably, as the two groups looked at each other, both felt betrayed.

Life at the college and the principal's house returned to something of a normal state after this trauma. Pennar continued to struggle with the ever-deepening problems of the college in the face of the constant decline in the number of ordinands available, a reflection of the state of the Welsh churches. He was, at least, as busy as ever, writing prose and poetry, politically active, serving the churches and struggling to raise a family on a pittance.

11

Independence
at all Costs

THE PROBLEMS FACING the college (of which the causes of the strike was but one symptom), were enormous, long-standing and refused to go away. In 1954 there was a quinquennial Visitation of theological colleges on behalf of the University of Wales. The task of the visitors was to ensure that the teaching and provision offered by all the colleges reached an appropriate standard. Four eminent men came to Brecon on 25 March 1954, a Scottish Presbyterian, Principal John Baillie[1] of Edinburgh; an English Anglican, Canon L W Grensted[2] of Oxford; the English Methodist biblical scholar, Dr Vincent Taylor[3] (nicknamed 'fifty shilling tailor' after the gentlemen's outfitters, because all his books seemed to cost that sum) and a Welsh Presbyterian, Dr J R Jones,[4] Professor of Philosophy at University College, Swansea.

The students had been informed in advance of the visitation, with some suggestions of its importance, though no one admitted to the senate's palpable fear of the visitors being dissatisfied with what they saw. They would not get a happy picture: the college was far from both the main centres of population and of theological learning, the buildings were in a deplorable state, money was very scarce, and entry standards were certainly being lowered in order to ensure adequate numbers. As for the teaching, a staff of four was expected to cover the whole range of theological education and, of them, only two made the grade in the students' eyes. College salaries were grossly inadequate, even when compared with the generally poor stipends of Congregational and Independent ministers in Wales.

In a letter to D Gethin Williams, the college's treasurer, dated 9 March 1959, Pennar wrote, "Principal Joseph Jones [on college staff, 1907–50] used to say that during the first period of his service at the college, the principal's salary was equivalent to that of a university professor and a professor's salary was equivalent to that of a senior lecturer in the university. Now that has completely changed." Power and status had gone too – the kind often exercised by bishops in other traditions, and accompanied, certainly at Brecon, by political muscle. In the 1950s students heard oft-repeated tales of Principal Joe's power in the community, which was summed up in the story of mail delivery: If the postman had not arrived by 8.30 a.m., Joe would phone the postmaster at Brecon, and say: "Joseph Jones here. The mail has not arrived. It is 8.30. I shall be out of morning prayers by 8.45." His mail and that of the students was always by the front door as they came from prayers – a van would be sent to take the college mail from the local postman. By 1954 this had all gone and with it much of the traditional respect for the ministry and those who served in it.

The college's problems were merely symptoms of a growing spiritual crisis. The writing was on the wall for the college in Brecon. The visitors' report was eventually published. It recommended the adoption of the federal pattern found at Bangor since 1922, which brought together the university's Department of Biblical Studies, the Baptist College, the Independents' Coleg Bala-Bangor and the Church Hostel (Church in Wales). The only place in south Wales which could match Bangor was Cardiff, with its Department of Semitic Languages and Cardiff Baptist College. (Several decades were to pass before a link developed with St Michael's, Llandaff.) In accepting the report, a move to Cardiff would be necessary for the two southern institutions which trained candidates for the Independent/Congregational ministry – Brecon and the Presbyterian College, Carmarthen.

Pennar's opposition was adamant. He made a scathing response at a meeting of the Faculty of Theology in May 1955, attacking every clause in the report: "The visitors... are erudite and worthy scholars who are ignorant of our Welsh institution and totally ignorant of the theological work done in the Welsh language."[5] He condemned their plan as "naïve". However, the comments of the visitors on standards were only too painfully accurate; if anyone was being naïve, it was the Brecon principal. Pennar and his colleagues could brook no outside interference from university departments in their life and work. Many of the Welsh Independent supporters of the colleges at Brecon and Carmarthen favoured a merger and a move to Swansea. Pennar also felt that Swansea was the best option at the time, and the importance of the west Wales chapels couldn't be underestimated in his view. He had a passionate interest in Carmarthenshire in particular and had written a study of the county's history and culture. Swansea, at the time, may already have been Anglicised but the hinterland was very much Welsh-speaking and had many Annibynwyr (Independent/Congregational) chapels, some of the most famous in the denomination's history. This was a consideration despite the risks involved in any move. The denomination's headquarters are still in Swansea, now based at the Glanyrafon Business Park.

Tensions were clear at the annual subscribers' meeting in Brecon, which followed weeks of canvassing by various 'parties': a Cardiff federal pattern was favoured by most ministers and representatives of the English-language churches and by those Welsh Independents whose primary concern was for academic standards and proper training, including several newly ordained, Brecon-trained graduates. It was Swansea which won the day – a grave error in the eyes of this former student, from which the college never recovered. A meeting of Brecon subscribers held at Neath on 10 April 1959 approved the union of the Congregational Memorial College with the Presbyterian College, Carmarthen, in Swansea, with Pennar as its principal. Two other members of staff were appointed, D P Roberts[6] (New Testament and Greek) of Carmarthen, and D L Trefor Evans,[7] who served both colleges since the retirement of Vernon Lewis.

The decision to move to Swansea and the events leading up to it were not without pain: Pennar was deeply hurt and caused hurt. At the time of the Brecon strike it was Pennar and Isaac who were held in the greatest respect for their teaching ability and they had become firm friends. Densil Morgan describes Isaac Thomas as upright and courteous, an Independent by conviction and an academic of the first rank.[8] The students of the early 1950s shared the admiration and respect given to Pennar and Isaac, but not the affection, as Isaac was not as easy to get along with. It became clear to Isaac Thomas that the two south Wales colleges would unite and that there would be need for only one Professor of New Testament. He had already changed subjects once to create a place for Pennar at Brecon.

So, in 1958, he applied for and was appointed to the post of lecturer in Biblical Studies at University College, Bangor. Pennar received the news with a sense of betrayal and bitterness. He made his response in a poem entitled 'Y Capten Coll' [The lost captain], which appeared in the winter 1958 issue of the literary magazine, Y Genhinen. It began: "He left us for a handful of gold, for some old trappings to show the world. He had what we were without, and became silent. He paid through losing all our treasures."[9] It was clear to everyone that Isaac Thomas was "the Backslider who was lost". In a letter to the college treasurer, Pennar wrote, "Professor Isaac Thomas is abandoning the cause of the ministry in the present crisis to enjoy comparative ease and affluence in a solely academic position".[10] This devastating condemnation was written of his colleague and friend, the man who had given up the teaching of Church History to make way for Pennar and taken on the subjects New Testament and Greek, with all the extra work of preparation that involved, together with the realisation that the newcomer would become principal, a role which, in other circumstances might have come to him. He must have been blinded to the situation of the other by the pain he suffered, caused by the recent traumatic events at the college. Something will be said later of the 'dark side' of this saintly man's character but there is a pointer to it here and a suggestion that the misanthropy which damaged his life as a young man had not completely left him.

The split between them was never healed, despite Isaac Thomas' willingness to praise his former colleague. As for Pennar, 'Y Capten Coll' was never included in any of his collections of poems, nor did he ever make any public reference either to the poem or the occasion of its composition. Pennar often expressed disappointment when he heard of ministers leaving the ministry for better paid jobs in other fields. A number left the industry from the 1960s onwards to work in the media industry. Pennar could be quite scathing about their decision to take the money and run – it wasn't quite akin to accepting thirty pieces of silver, but close to it.

The new united college moved into its new home, a large house in the Ffynnone district of Swansea, in readiness for the autumn term of 1959. In so doing it lost the student accommodation available in Brecon, with a consequent weakening of a sense of community.

12

Bow with many Strings

THE DAVIES FAMILY soon settled in its new home, with four children (aged between three and thirteen) and a fifth, Cei Owen, born in 1961. For the first time Pennar was able to spend real time with his family. The one sad note was the death of Pennar's mother in March 1961 at the age of 81; her passing marked the end of an era in her son's life. The 1960s were a busy time for Pennar. He found himself nearer the strength of Welsh Independency in south-west Wales. He had won his place in several fields and his opinion counted in literary and religious circles.

His lifelong friend, J Gwyn Griffiths, admits to being uncertain about how Pennar Davies became a member of Plaid Cymru:

He greatly admired Saunders Lewis.[1] Gwynfor Evans had a particular and direct influence upon him, arising to some extent from their friendship and interchange of ideas. The likelihood is that his early attachment to the nationalist cause began as a natural result of his interest in our culture... A quick look at his contribution to the nationalist movement reveals that he constantly offered himself as a public speaker, a parliamentary candidate, as an editor and writer. As a public speaker it was natural for him to reveal the same gifts as he used as a preacher. He brought together reason and enthusiasm, historical commentary and contemporary appeal, here was the secret of his strength. Yes, light and warmth. Like Gwynfor Evans he is fond of turning often to the rich sources of the history of Wales. One of Pennar's favourite themes is the honourable place given to woman in the life of Wales, and that far before the coming of modern times... He serves his nation and his society with humility and self-sacrifice; Pennar has done this constantly and still does it. He has gladly rejected those material luxuries which could easily have been his had he not chosen another path. As part of his contribution to the national cause he has been willing to take on those tasks which are really hard work... I dare to say that our national movement is one in which we can rejoice, and do so because its roots like its methods are Christian... People like Pennar Davies have made this possible... [2]

Nonetheless, though zealous in his support for Plaid Cymru, Pennar was not a natural politician, probably becoming a candidate through the pressure of his close friend, Gwynfor Evans.[3] Nontheless it was with enthusiasm and a strong sense of duty and commitment that he contested the Llanelli constituency for the party in 1964 and 1966 (for details, see Appendix IV). Pennar stood against the veteran Labour statesman, Jim Griffiths, himself of Welsh Independent stock. In his election address to the voters of Llanelli in the general election of 1966, Pennar wrote:

By your vote you can make a vast difference to the future of your town, of your county and of Wales. If you vote for one of the big London-based political parties, you will do nothing to help your people; for their policies condemn Wales to be a dying fringe territory to the west of England's wealthy economic belt. If you vote for Plaid Cymru, the Welsh Party, you will show that you want Wales, your own Country, to live.

Every vote counts. A substantial and encouraging vote for the only Welsh Party is bound to affect the outlook of any government that may gain power. Our aims as a Party are fair and just; our methods are peaceable. We have good will to the English, the Scots, the Irish and all our neighbours. Our motto is 'Live and let live'.

In the past the Welsh people have done much for world peace, for democracy, for things of the mind, for the betterment of the common people. We are the heirs of this radical tradition. Let us give it a new and vital expression in a modern and self-reliant Wales. Let Cambria, one of the oldest nations of Europe, take its place with other nations, old and new, in the quest for a world order in accordance with the values we have inherited.[4]

Although he never became an important historian – like his friend Geoffrey Nuttall, his Bangor successor, Tudur Jones or his next-door neighbour in Swansea, Glanmor Williams,[5] Pennar's firm grip on and keen discernment of Church History were accompanied by a particular interest in two periods, the early Celtic Church[6] and Protestantism from the Puritans onwards. He addressed the Welsh Independents History Society on the link between religion and literature in the Cromwellian period. His *Episodes in the History of Brecknockshire Dissent* (1957) was warmly received by historians across Offa's Dyke, whilst his booklet *John Penry* (1961) was intended to present one of Wales' great heroes to an English audience. In this and other works he reveals himself as more the interpreter than the researcher. The 1962 *Llyfr Gwasanaeth* [Service book] published by the Union of Welsh Independents, contains a wealth of prayers collected by Pennar down the years from old liturgies. Clearly the spiritual life continued to appeal to him, even though he had turned from the High Congregationalism he had espoused in the 1940s. Rosemary's Lutheranism influenced him too. His *Rhwng Chwedl a Chredo* [Between fable and creed] (1966) sought to "reconsider certain aspects of our literature and history from a theological standpoint" and "to trace the fusing of Celtic paganism with old Christianity among the ancient Welsh". Pennar's great hero is Pelagius, the fourth/fifth-century Christian ascetic whose theology emphasised performing good works above grace and divine aid. In Pennar's view, Pelagius brings together every theological virtue and gives expression to the religious genius of the Welsh before it was corrupted by Roman Augustinianism and the Calvinism which developed out of it.

All the while he continued to fill his life with numerous

interests and activities. He was the first Nonconformist to be invited to address *Y Cylch Catholig* (the prestigious Catholic Circle) in August 1966. He continued to be a prodigious letter writer. His two closest friends were J Gwyn Griffiths and Gwynfor Evans. Then there was a close, loyal relationship with Clem Linnenberg, from his Yale days. Pennar dedicated his book, *Caregl Nwyf*, to Clem and his wife, Marianne, sending them an English précis of its contents. A fourth close friend was the Congregationalist and distinguished church historian, Geoffrey Nuttall. A long correspondence began between them in the 1950s and Nuttall, of all of them, was the boldest in his comments, never fearing to offer what he regarded as justified criticism. He frequently complained at Pennar's failure to contribute to international scholarship and for his failure to be involved in denominational affairs on a British level. He always added bits of gossip about the Oxford colleges and dealt with academic and religious interests common to them.

This all went on against a background of a changing Wales. The politically seismic election result at Carmarthen in 1966, which saw the election of Gwynfor Evans as the first Plaid Cymru MP, gave a new impetus to the nationalist cause. At the same time, more impatient voices were weary of the long and slow constitutional process and turning to direct, non-violent action in their battle to save the Welsh language and culture. The Welsh Language Society, Cymdeithas yr Iaith had been formed following a powerful radio lecture by Saunders Lewis on the future of the language. The first protest on the question of the legal status of Welsh, mainly by young people, took place outside Aberystwyth Post Office before moving to the town's Trefechan Bridge. Pennar made his support public and he was one of two leading figures invited to address a Cymdeithas rally at Cefn Brith, the home of the first Congregationalist martyr, John Penry. Although there was a religious element in his words, the main emphasis was political. By the end of the decade he was regarded as being clearly in the camp of radical politics, for which he would be held to account. The Memorial

College served English- as well as Welsh-language churches and Pennar was on the roll of ministers of both congregations.

Tensions in Wales grew as the proposed 1969 investiture of the heir to the throne as Prince of Wales, an idea strongly supported by George Thomas,[7] Labour MP and later Speaker of the House of Commons, whose hatred of all that Plaid Cymru represented was vitriolic in the extreme. A royal occasion would dazzle the people of Wales and make them forget such foolishness. In 1963 Pennar had become president of the Free Church Council of Wales, and, as such, was expected to represent all opinions in its member denominations. He worthily expressed the sadness and sympathy of the churches to the people of Aberfan in October 1966, when a generation of children in that mining village near Merthyr Tydfil, in the next valley to Mountain Ash, was wiped out when a neglected coal tip swept through the school. This was to do with his own suffering people.

Now he was to be challenged by a clash between his role and his principles. This crisis came about with an official letter from none other than the Duke of Norfolk, Earl Marshal of England, inviting him to join the Investiture Planning Committee. His sense of duty took Pennar to the first meeting at St James's Palace but his conscience was far from happy. In an undated letter to Gwynfor Evans, he pours out his heart: "My fellow nationalists are already calling me a traitor because I sit on the investiture committee with such worthy men, from Jim Griffiths and Cynan down to Glanmor Williams and little Ednyfed, as well as English lords and court officials."[8] Although Gwynfor set great store by Pennar's presence on the committee, Pennar himself could not stick it – the military pomp and ceremony, reflecting for him the power of English imperialism, was more than he could stomach. Later he wrote that the main purpose in investing the son of the Queen of England as Prince of Wales "is to enthrone Britishness rather than Welshness in the consciousness of the Welsh people. It is a device to weaken the national feeling which has grown so much in Wales during this century. John Bull, with his little servant Dic Sion Dafydd[9] has thrust the Investiture upon us. Every true Welshman must reject this attempt to enslave and corrupt the minds of our people."[10] On 18 March 1968, he informed the officers of the Free Church Council of Wales of his decision to resign as president: "I am emphatically not a suitable person to represent the Free Church Council of Wales in the investiture of the Prince of Wales and the committees that are preparing for it" – a statement that would not endear him to many people within the churches.

Densil Morgan reminds us that Pennar had a slow start as an artist and scholar. His youth was swallowed up by his research into English literature during the reign of Elizabeth I. His change of direction at the outbreak of the Second World War gave him a new beginning in the fields of religion and theology and he had reached middle age before making a recognised contribution in these disciplines. It is remarkable that with his many responsibilities in the world of theology, education, politics and literature that his energies did not fail. Quite the contrary! As he approached retirement age, his activities increased and deepened. Clem Linnenberg wrote on 23 August 1969, "I admire what you have done with your life and what you have achieved with it".[11]

Pennar gave new treatment to his favoured themes of religion and nationalism during this period. Although his links with English Congregationalism were almost broken, he wrote a chapter entitled 'God's Universe' in *Christian Confidence*, published to mark Nathaniel Micklem's eightieth birthday: "The hope lies not in the powers of mankind but in the promise of God, not in a city built by the resources of a self-sufficient humanity, but in a city which is given to the saints by the Most High, not in a gradual advance towards perfection but in a victory won over sin... The promise of a time of tribulation seems not ill-founded." In 1974 Micklem wrote to him after re-reading the book whilst on holiday: "I have been re-reading to my great comfort and at a greater leisure your contribution to *Christian Confidence*. It is a mighty utterance and makes me wish that I and my fellow pilgrims could manage Welsh that we might read what you have written in prose and poetry."[12]

13

Poetry and Prose

HIS FIRST COLLECTION of poems was published in the Anglo-Welsh anthology, *Modern Welsh Poetry*, edited by Keidrych Rhys, in 1944. Pennar's writings showed how and why he parted company with the Swansea poets. Whereas Pennar sought to challenge the grimness of life at the time for so many people, Dylan Thomas and Vernon Watkins showed neither spiritual or political commitment. In *Artists in Wales* he explained his decision to write in Welsh in these terms: "To accept the vocation of Welsh artist is not, of course, to part company with the world. The Welsh writer, curiously enough, enjoys the freedom of the literary seas in a fuller sense than his Anglo-Welsh counterpart, for the Anglo-Welsh author is in danger of losing his Welsh character unless he writes 'about Wales'... but when I published in Welsh, stories about a Spanish nun and a Soviet scientist, no one suggested I was the less Welsh for doing so." He had to accept this vocation in face of "the agonizing crisis of the language", adding later, "the crisis of Wales mirrors the crisis of the world".

Poetry was his first love and there was newness and a freshness – to put it mildly – which was prominent in his work from the beginning. Some people were shocked by the title he chose for his first volume in 1949 – *Cinio'r Cythraul* [The devil's dinner] – using the name Davies Aberpennar. He was a minister at the time and about to be appointed professor of Church History at Bala-Bangor College. It would have been more natural, perhaps, to expect a title like 'Te'r Tystion'

[The witnesses' tea] or 'Swper y Saint' [The saints' supper]. But *Cinio'r Cythraul* was his ardent choice. Some fearful and conservative Welsh Independents were concerned about the fate of the innocent students of Bala-Bangor. These frightened doubters were not aware that he chose the title on the basis of the early theology of the Church which speaks of the devil being caught on a hook hidden in bait; the hook was divinity and the humanity of Jesus was the bait. This poem contains an element of satire and laughter alongside the contrast between flesh and spirit. The poem's last two lines are:

> Gan bwyll: mae Duw wedi cuddio'r Bachyn
> Dan ffolineb y cerddi damniol hyn.

> (Take care: God has hidden the Hook
> Within the foolishness of these damning poems.)[1]

This was Pennar's romantic period. In reviewing the volume *Y Fflam* [The flame] (1946) Saunders Lewis suggested that he was not such a rebel as some believed: "A young poet is singing – he is 35... I heard some people complain that the book is dark and difficult, too clever and too learned. Well, cleverness and learning belong to the young and if learning and cleverness can sing there is no need to complain or find fault... The book contains promise."

Pennar Davies Cyfrol Deyrnged (1981), a volume paying tribute to Pennar was published under the editorship of his colleague, Dewi Eurig Davies. Gilbert Ruddock, a fellow poet, who also learned Welsh, and was a lecturer in Welsh at Cardiff, wrote in his article entitled, 'Menter ac Antur, Cariad a Hedd' [Venture and adventure, love and peace]:

> The main themes of Pennar Davies' poetry may be thus listed: religion, love, mythology, his country, his childhood days, art – and so too with his most obvious attributes, such as rich references, the fondness for symbolism and the ironic touch, and effective and striking cadences. In reading his creative literary works, and especially his poetry, one is struck by the unity, the consistency of thought and attitude which runs through it all.[2]

In the same book John Rowlands writes of 'Y Llenor Enigmatig' [The enigmatic literary man]:

> Who knows what various inducements lead someone to turn to Welsh? Does not a youth with some adventure in his blood turn to Europe and the world. Stepping across the threshold of Welsh can appear as an escape to a little, comfortable hearth, and an opportunity for an introverted person to tread the stairs down to the cellar to search among the relics of the past and feel safe. But Pennar Davies does not fit into that frame at all. There is in him, though young, no lack of mental adventure. He studied, not only in the University of Wales, but also at Oxford and then at Yale University in the United States. It was only after regarding the world that he turned back to look at Wales and to look upon her through the spectacles of the Welsh language.[3]

Rowlands continues:

> I would not dare suggest for a moment that it was a mistake for Pennar to turn to Welsh. Though the penetrating comments of Gareth Alban Davies in the volume *Dyrnaid o Awduron Cyfoes* [A handful of contemporary authors] are so intelligible, I cannot agree with him when he says, "this poet would have been finer, more sure of himself, if he had continued to sing in the English language". It must be accepted that this may be true for the occasional poet, but the feeling I get is that caressing his second language gave Pennar Davies the opportunity to distance himself from the baseness of his background, and that this was congenial to his personality. Welsh was for him a door opening into the land of imagination. This did not mean the recovering of tradition, as far as I can see, because what strikes us about this writer is *how different* he is – from the Welsh as well as the Anglo-Welsh viewpoint. Adopting Welsh as his medium was an act of estranging himself and in estranging himself he found freedom – the freedom to be odd in a culture where oddness would shine. I am not suggesting that Pennar Davies distorted his gift in choosing to create in his second language, but, rather that he found the true nature of his own genius as a man of letters.[4]

14

Protests

THE WELSH LANGUAGE Society's campaign was growing and, by the end of the 1960s, scores, if not hundreds of its members had appeared before magistrates' courts for their campaigns to secure official status for the Welsh language. Pennar, as one of the older people involved in the campaign, was the object of some admiration and much criticism. In April 1971 he was one of a group of ministers who covered an English road sign at Carmarthen with its Welsh equivalent. Some weeks later he was among some 2,000 people outside Swansea Crown Court, when eight members of the Welsh Language Society stood trial on a charge of conspiring to remove English road signs. Before the end of the day scores of protesters were arrested, among them the prominent academic and broadcaster Dr Meredydd Edwards of Bangor and Pennar Davies of Swansea. Gilbert Ruddock, the poet and critic from Cardiff, wrote to Pennar expressing his "pride and admiration of you last Saturday... this was a historic occasion and there you were in the middle of it all giving leadership and an example to everyone".[1]

There were many people who took a contrary view, not least in the English churches of south Wales. The Congregational churches at Crundale and Wolfsdale in Pembrokeshire broke their links with the college: "It was unanimously decided to convey to you the great distress which all the members feel at your recent public actions in support of pseudo-political activities connected with the Welsh Language Society... To support violence, subversion, malicious damage and similar

Pennar Davies's family portrait taken in January 1915

photo: Pennar Davies's family

Pennar with his mother Edith, around 1923

photo: Pennar Davies's family

Pennar with Edith, around 1930

photo: Pennar Davies's family

Balliol College, Oxford which Pennar attended 1934–6

Pennar's fellow students at Balliol College, 1935

photo: Pennar Davies's family

Yale University, Connecticut, which Pennar attended 1936–9

Pennar's room at Yale

photo: Pennar Davies's family

Pennar with Ted Taylor on their 3,300-mile road trip around the United States

photo: Pennar Davies's family

Friends J Gwyn Griffiths and Käthe Bosse's wedding in 1939
photo: Heini Gruffudd

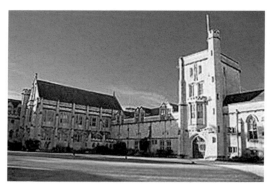

Mansfield College, Oxford University,
which Pennar attended 1941–3

MANSFIELD COLLEGE J.C.R., 1942

GEORGE WILLIAMS   PETER SCOTT   'PETER' BROOKS   GEORGE CAIRD   CYRIL LLOYD   BILL DAVIES
BASIL SIMS   ERIK ROUTLEY   TONY HALL   PHILIP LEE WOOLF
EDGAR YOUDELL   HORTON DAVIES   'AL' BEEZLEY   DR. HIRSCHWALD   G. D. BOAZ   TOM HAWTHORN   JIM HARDIMAN   BOB PAUL

Mansfield College Junior Common Room, 1942
illustration: Pennar Davies's family

MANSFIELD COLLEGE S.C.R.

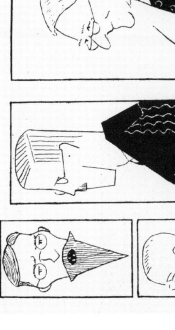
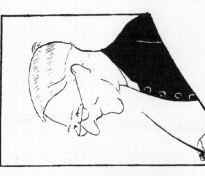
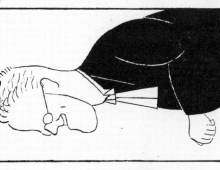

W.E.H. O.Vi.1943.

REVD. A. M. HUNTER, M.A., B.D., PH.D., D.PHIL.,
YATES PROFESSOR OF NEW TESTAMENT THEOLOGY

REVD. C. J. CADOUX, M.A., D.D., D.LITT.,
MACKENNAL PROFESSOR OF CHURCH HISTORY

REVD. JOHN MARSH, M.A.
CHAPLAIN

REVD. NATHANIEL MICKLEM, M.A., D.D., LL.D
THE PRINCIPAL

REVD. H. WHEELER ROBINSON, M.A., D.D.
PRINCIPAL OF REGENT'S PARK COLLEGE

REVD. W. H. CADMAN, B.D., B.LITT., D.THEOL.
RESEARCH FELLOW

REV. J. H. MILNES. M.A.
BURSAR

Mansfield College Senior Common Room, showing some of Pennar's tutors

illustration: Pennar Davies's family

Pennar's wife-to-be, Rosemarie Wolff, in a nurse's uniform at Oxford

photo: Pennar Davies's family

Minster Road Church, Cardiff. Pennar was ordained here in July 1943

photo: courtesy of Parkminster United Reformed Church, Cardiff

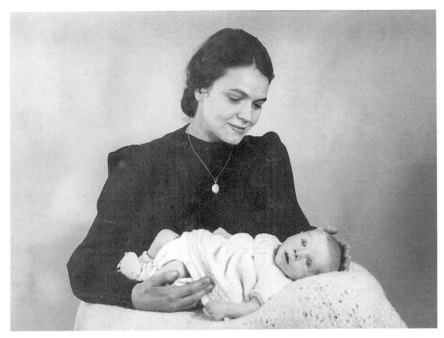

Rosemarie with son Meirion, who was born in 1944

photo: Pennar Davies's family

Pennar, Rosemarie and Meirion

photo: Pennar Davies's family

Bala-Bangor College, where Pennar was appointed Professor of Church History in 1946

photo: Dafydd Tudur

Pennar and Rosemarie's children, Rhiannon and Geraint, around 1954

Pennar with Meirion, around 1947

photo: Pennar Davies's family

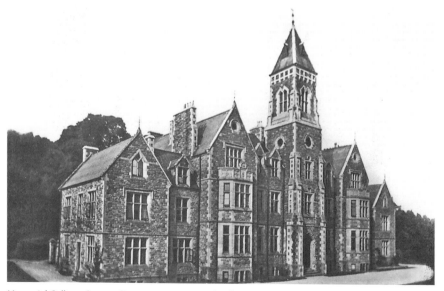

Memorial College, Brecon. Pennar was appointed college principal in 1952

Rev. Prof. Isaac Thomas
B.A., B.D.

Rev. Principal
Dr. W. T. Pennar-Davies
B.A., B.Litt. Ph.D.

Rev. Prof.
J. Vernon Lewis
M.A., B.D.

Rev. Prof. D. J. Davies
B.A.

Memorial College staff, 1954–5

Students of Memorial College, Brecon, 1953–4

Pennar with the students after the strike in 1955

L–R 4th row: John MacLaughlan, David Bowen
3rd row: Dyrinos Thomas, Lionel Walker, Dewi Lloyd Lewis, William Jones, Gwyn Rhys, Brychan Davies
2nd row: Luther Rees, Keith Phillips, Derek Churchward, Sam Williams, Maldwyn Mundy, Reg Williams, Kenneth Stork
Front row: Jean Wilkinson, Aeron Davies, David Morris, Gerald Smith, Pennar Davies, John Evans, Ivor Rees,
Fred Williams, John Wilstead

Rosemarie with all the children, around 1962
photo: Heini Gruffudd

The Pennar and Griffiths families gather together in Swansea
photo: Heini Gruffudd

Pennar with J Gwyn and Kate Griffiths
photo: Heini Gruffudd

Meirion Pennar
photo: Pennar Davies's family

Memorial College exhibition in Swansea

photo: Heini Gruffudd

Pennar Davies in 1977

photo: Pennar Davies's family

anti-social activities, to whatever object these activities be directed, is not in line with the Christian ethic, and brings the Church, your college and yourself into disrepute."[2] The news of the tensions between English Congregationalists in south Wales and Memorial College reached the ears of Geoffrey Nuttall, who wrote saying, "If anyone deserved admiration and loyalty from the Welsh, it is surely you, who have given yourself so entirely and unselfishly to Wales' best interests."[3] Pennar's response came in a vigil at the time of the Swansea trial, recorded in an undated paper: "There was a feeling that at last the people of Wales are awakening to the fact that they have moral power to claim the right to use their own language for all the purposes of modern life... The conviction emerged that the tradition of Christian faith in Wales, going back over the centuries, was now identifying itself with the struggles of the language which was the chief medium of Christian communication in Wales throughout the ages."

In his presidential address to the Union of Welsh Independents in June 1973 on 'Y Pethau nad Ydynt' [The things that are not], Pennar expressed his concern that so many newly enthusiastic Welsh people were outside both the chapels and the influence of Christianity, and the fault for that lay with the lukewarm Christians of the Nonconformist establishment. He was troubled that so many believers had turned their backs on "the great adventure of the world to come" and the "challenge of the eschatological hope". The fullness of the glory of the Kingdom of God lies in the future, not in the past: "Our task, by the grace of God, is to prepare the world to see the fulfilling of the heavenly vision, the new heaven and the new earth." Turning back from this dazzling, apocalyptic vision to the question of uniting churches was like moving from the activity of life to a cemetery.

There were ecumenical challenges to be faced. The Congregational Church in England and Wales and the Presbyterian Church of England were moving towards union. R Tudur Jones was anxious to get Pennar to join his crusade against the proposed United Reformed Church.[4] Pennar did have much sympathy with this view and mourned the demise of Congregationalism in England. However, to R Tudur Jones's bitter disappointment, his fellow principal declined. What really mattered to Pennar was the essence of the faith itself. The theological excitement of the 1960s had come from Bishop John Robinson and his cry that "the world had come of age" and the disciples of Rudolph Bultmann's concern to de-mythologise the New Testament. In Wales, Pennar's friend, J R Jones, the first Christian to be appointed Professor of Philosophy at Swansea, had made known his own radical ideas, deeply influencing Pennar's own thoughts, which found expression in his book, *Y Brenin Alltud* [The exiled king], published in 1974.

Pennar's theologising was happening against a background of quite exciting political developments. The Labour government, led by James Callaghan, promised a referendum on devolution. The enthusiasm of John Morris, MP for Aberavon and Secretary of State for Wales, was shared by few people in the Labour Party. Although Gwynfor Evans now led a parliamentary party of three members, the heady days of Welsh nationalism, following the Gwynfor Evans victory at Carmarthen, were over. At the same time theological thought was moving away from the middle ground. Pennar and R Tudur Jones never allowed their theological differences to damage their friendship but each was subjected to attack from other quarters, with evangelicals subjecting the Swansea principal to scathing criticism, whilst prominent liberals attacked R Tudur Jones, whose guidance had made Bangor a centre of the Calvinist revival. The differences between Pennar Davies and R Tudur Jones were at the heart of the Welsh Independents denomination and its Union (Undeb yr Annibynwyr) in the latter part of the twentieth century. There were major differences between both men's theology that probably would have made a united college at that time almost impossible. He felt that the literal unquestioning interpretation of the Bible was impossible to believe, and, that only a liberal interpretation of the Bible emphasising the historical Jesus as a man among his people, could be relevant and believable. He felt that R Tudur Jones' theology was directing the denomination dangerously, in his view, towards evangelicalism. However, the two great theologians also had many meeting points. Pennar had the greatest respect for Tudur's academic brilliance and unyielding faith. R Tudur Jones' preface to the reprint of Pennar's confessional diary showed a similar respect for the man that some would perhaps consider his rival. Their main meeting point was that they were both committed Christians, convinced that God had come to the world in the embodiment of Christ. Pennar, in later life in particular, developed an interest in the works of Karl Barth, a theologian which interested Tudur greatly too. Barth argued that the belief that Christ is the Word of God did not have to necessarily depend on the belief that everything written in the Bible was historically and scientifically accurate. Here perhaps was a place where the two theological thinkers could have met.

However, it was literature and not theology which was Pennar's great interest at this time. In 1976 he made a rare visit to London at Geoffrey Nuttall's behest to deliver the 'Drew Lecture on Immortality' to an audience of United Reformed Church and Congregational Church members and the London Welsh. Nuttall's comments were typically forthright: "Your lecture was rather Celtic in its lack of architectonic – I hope that your university lecture in January will have a firmer and closer structure – but how full it was of shafts of insight as well as your own incomparable combination of wide reading and confident faith."[5]

In the same year he was awarded an Arts Council of Wales scholarship, which enabled him to take a sabbatical and work on a novel. This was but an all too brief escape from the college and its ever-growing problems. The supply of students was drying up and their intellectual calibre was dropping. The ministry had virtually lost its status and had no appeal for the best of the churches' young people, especially within the Nonconformist ministry. The academic and administrative burdens of the college fell on the principal's shoulders and he was often almost overwhelmed by it all. The departure of Professor Maurice Loader to return to the pastoral ministry left a serious gap as no one could be found among the Welsh Independents to teach Greek and New Testament.

Pennar himself was 67 in 1978 and due for retirement, but there was no church historian in sight to take his place. Worst of all, he and Rosemary faced an enormous financial crisis. They had no money and nowhere to go. He told the college officers that:

> ... we raised five children. Though the college did its best for its professors, my income was never sufficient to do more than support the family from day to day, leaving nothing over. I am not complaining: I had satisfaction and pleasure in my work. I refused a post in University College, Aberystwyth, to come to this work and I refused the possibility of a post at Mansfield College, Oxford, but I have never regretted that. I am grateful to have had the opportunity to give this sort of service in Wales. But I should like to feel that we shall have a home to go to when I retire.[6]

15

Aberystwyth

A MEASURE OF relief was afforded to the college principal in October 1977 by the decision to move the college to Aberystwyth, to become part of the new faculty of theology serving the university colleges at Aberystwyth and Lampeter. No one at the time commented that this was the same pattern as was suggested in the plan (which was so forcefully rejected), to move from Brecon to Cardiff. The new arrangement meant that the biblical subjects could be taught by the staff at the Presbyterian College, leaving Pennar with Church History and the Rev. Dewi Eurig Davies, appointed in 1970 to succeed D J Davies, being responsible for Christian Doctrine. This was the best that could be hoped for in such difficult circumstances. Pennar, who was due to retire in 1979, agreed to stay on for an extra year. He, Rosemary and son Geraint moved into the house purchased for them in Grosvenor Road, Swansea, in December 1979. For the next two years he made the slow and arduous road journey from Swansea to Aberystwyth to lecture, the last year without pay.

The move to Swansea and then Aberystwyth meant that there were now only two Welsh Independent Colleges, Swansea and Bala-Bangor. The relationship between the principals of the two Independent colleges was complex. They were the two outstanding scholars among the leading figures in Welsh Independency. Despite their mutual respect they held very different views on both Christianity and the Congregationalist tradition. In an article on Congregationalism in the 1981 edition of the Welsh theological journal, *Diwinyddiaeth*, Pennar wrote that: "Whereas the principal of Bangor is a 'classicist', I tend to be... a bit of a 'romanticist', seeing Congregationalism not in terms of order and tradition but in the freedom of the Spirit." As early as 18 November 1963, there were thoughts that Bangor and Memorial College should merge – as is shown in a letter from R Tudur Jones to Pennar: "I had a long conversation with Gwilym Bowyer [principal of Bangor] who said that his successor would need to seriously consider the appropriateness of uniting Bangor and Memorial College." When he succeeded Bowyer as principal two years later, there were those who thought it was time to close the northern college, but R Tudur Jones was not ready for this. He returned to the theme of uniting the colleges again in two letters[1] in 1966 but then, in a letter dated 14 November 1973, he admitted that the thought of moving from Bangor created a personal difficulty for him: "The work we are doing here is flourishing. There is no shortage of applications for a place here. And applications are beginning to come from young people of a high academic standard."

In 1973 too there was disagreement over the opening of college doors to Unitarians. Through his orthodox stand Dr R Tudur Jones nurtured for himself an enthusiastic following among evangelicals inside and outside the Union of Welsh Independents, probably without intending it. Believers of an evangelical persuasion would turn to him for advice and that surfaced in 1973 when Pennar Davies opened the doors of Memorial College, Swansea, to Unitarians. Pennar was adamant that the Unitarians should be welcomed into the Memorial College. He considered the almost heretical denomination as an important part of the Welsh religious tradition and felt that their inclusion would widen and inform the theological debate at the college. He realised the risk involved in alienating and offending the conservative wing of his own denomination, but felt it was worthwhile in the pursuit of knowledge. It showed a tendency in Pennar to push the boundaries in his faith. Dr Elwyn Davies, the nephew of one of Wales's most famous Unitarian ministers, D Jacob Davies, became a close colleague of Pennar's when he joined the college staff. For some, it was akin to supping with the devil.

Once more Noel Gibbard shared his concern on this matter with Tudur Jones: "One of the professors and three students are Unitarian", said Gibbard. "Not many churches are aware of this." Noel Gibbard[2] and his fellow officers at Llanelli decided that they would not receive Unitarians to their pulpit. The same opposition was expressed by Independents of an evangelical persuasion in Merioneth – John and Mari Jones wrote to the principal of Coleg Bala-Bangor from Llanymawddwy to express horror at the students who came to fill pulpits in their district. "One who came was a Unitarian", stated John and Mari Jones, adding that the student "denied the divinity of Christ". A fortnight later another student arrived from Swansea but the Independents of Llanymawddwy sent him packing back to Memorial College to explain their reasons in the most explicit way. "The public debates between Tudur Jones and Iorwerth Jones[3] reveal that Tudur Jones was the intelligent keeper of the classic evangelical faith within the ranks of Independency and Nonconformity in general during his period."[4] Ten years later, with the Memorial College now at Aberystwyth, many of its supporters, including Pennar, felt that Bangor was planning a takeover, so creating one Welsh Independent college with a conservative theology.

Despite these tensions the two principals shared a great concern for the nature and success of the Christian ministry and for the spiritual state of Wales. Clearly neither thought in terms of a Welsh Taizé or Iona, as Dewi Lloyd Lewis points out later. On Pennar's side, it may have been that he was weighed down with the matter of the future of the language and culture of Wales.

16

Retirement

PENNAR DAVIES FINALLY retired in 1981 when, at last, he was entitled to a state pension. His salary at retirement was £3,500 a year and his appointment as dean of the new faculty can have done little to ease his burdens. Densil Morgan comments: "A man of his experience and stature should have been able to look forward to a comfortable retirement and leisure at last to do what he wanted, with some means to do so. Sadly, a new chapter of discomfort with more hardship to come was about to open in his story."[1]

On the political stage there had been great changes. The 1979 devolution referendum on St David's Day was a disaster for those who sought home rule. Two months later the Conservatives gained power when Margaret Thatcher swept into Downing Street. One of the first actions of the new government was to renege on its promise to set aside a new fourth television channel for broadcasting in Welsh. A period of intense civil disobedience was dawning. In an article 'Ystyried Eiddo' [Considering property] in the journal *Y Faner* dated 2 February 1979, Pennar took a strong line, making a clear differentiation between violence against people and that against property. It is clear that between the spring and autumn, Pennar, Dr Meredydd Evans and Ned Thomas engaged in much thought and discussion. Ideas turned into action on the night of 11 October 1979 when these three men broke into the television transmitter at Pencarreg, Llanybydder, and turned off the machinery. Programmes were lost for about an hour before they were arrested. In his autobiography, *Bydoedd, Cofiant Cyfnod* [Worlds, portrait of a period], published in 2010, Ned Thomas provides a fascinating insight into the atmosphere surrounding the action, which caused so much anger within many sections of the public in both Wales and England:

> 11 October 1979. It is teatime and the best china is spread out on the parlour table. A very respectable couple, pillars of Llanybydder society, are passing around cups of tea to three respectable guests. The principal of Memorial College, Swansea, Pennar Davies, is the first. The second is a senior lecturer in the Extramural Department of University College, Cardiff, well known to everyone in Welsh-speaking Wales since his time at the BBC and as a performer on national platforms. This is Meredydd Edwards. I am the third, from a younger generation, having newly climbed to a higher step of respectability on my promotion to senior lecturer at University College, Aberystwyth. From time to time the heads of several students appear at the window. After nightfall the students' car leaves first and we follow after some ten minutes. We meet at the summit of Pencarreg mountain near the television transformer bearing that name. After they cut a hole in the fence and open the doors, the students disappear. It is we who are to turn off the transmitter, but that is not easy – there are so many complicated switches. Eventually we succeed in pressing the switch which stops the humming sound above our heads. After a long wait and while Pennar is in the middle of explaining the social and religious divisions of fifteenth-century Florence, two policemen arrive from Lampeter. One immediately recognises Merêd [Meredydd Evans] and the two begin to discuss a local eisteddfod at which Merêd was an adjudicator. We go voluntarily to Lampeter police station, where there was more discussion of eisteddfodau. After a long wait and much phoning, we are allowed to go home without any charge against us. We had expected a night in the cells.[2]

They were summoned to appear before Llandovery magistrates on a charge of burglary and criminal damage. It was an act which made headline news and divided opinion. This unlawful act is said to have inspired Gwynfor Evans (were Gwynfor and Rhiannon Evans 'the pillars of Llanybydder society' with whom they had tea before proceeding to Pencarreg?) in his decision to fast. It also caused some anguish in the Pennar Davies household at Memorial College, Swansea. Rosemarie, partly because of a fear of authority borne from her experiences in Nazi German and partly because of her Lutheran respect for authority, did not agree with his decision. Her love and affection for Pennar meant that she did support him during the subsequent trial, but it was difficult for her, especially as two of her sons, Meirion and Hywel, had also been involved in varying degrees in the language protest movement.

The news spread far and wide. Geoffrey Nuttall was among the first to make contact: "I have not heard a word from you but have read many words *about* you and your doings, which have distressed your friends in many parts, Welsh as well as English. I have tried to put as understanding a face on it as possible, but your behaviour (as reported) is hard to accept as approvable in a Christian, minister and pacifist, and I would *like* to excuse it as an expression of a temporary diversion through the pressures and anxieties you have been under as of late."[3] Nuttall was even more shaken by the brutal treatment given to Pennar by his acquaintances in England. He wrote again a week later expressing concern for his Welsh friend "during this period of your being publicly vilified... So, you see, I have been with you in a not wholly successful effort at 'sympathy' in this". Not every Plaid Cymru member supported him either, to Pennar's great disappointment. Jennie Eirian Davies, a former candidate for Carmarthen and now editor of the journal, *Y Faner*, opposed the idea of a separate Welsh channel on the grounds that it would separate Welsh speakers and non-Welsh speakers.[4]

The defendants appeared before Carmarthen Crown Court on 28 July. In his defence argued that: "A moral necessity compelled us to undertake the action which has brought us to this place to be tried before you." He told the court of his experiences as a Welsh learner and his ideals for the continuance of the nation and civilisation. He was a Christian and a pacifist, with a real respect for the law of the land, but he felt that in this instance he had no choice but to challenge that law:

> All my life's work has been based on the belief that God exists, the authority for creation and salvation, the Goodness, the Suffering and the unfettered Wind which blows in every truth and every beauty under heaven. For me there is no meaning to life apart from the conviction that the whole world is part of the Living God's adventure in which we are allowed to live, and that His is the Strength, Wisdom and Love which create and sustain it... I have reached retirement age and one of my comforts is my hope that I may have more time to write poetry and the occasional novel or article. I am one of the many who struggle to create literature through the medium the Welsh language. That language is now in grievous danger. To create literature one needs an audience. Publishing is pointless without a public. The publication of Welsh literature is being destroyed, the nation is being killed.[5]

This appeal had no effect and the three defendants were fined £2,000 each plus costs, an impossible sum for the poor pensioner. Geoffrey Nuttall kept in close touch, half angry with and half concerned for his friend: "What I envisage is that you will refuse [to pay], will then go to prison, and, after a day or two, will gratefully if reluctantly accept release, when the campaign and/or personal friends, have paid the fines for you. I shall *not* be among those who come to your rescue."[6] He went on to say that he would visit his friend in prison, assuring him of his affection and respect, adding: "I feel very torn between disapproval and difficulty in comprehension of your behaviour, and its effect on the family and on the young, regard for you in your following a painful course you believe to be right, and affection and concern for you, and Rosemarie, and your and her health physically and nervously." In the event, a fund for the paying of such fines had been established already. The point was made and Pennar was free.

During the period between the initial hearing before Llandovery magistrates and the case at Carmarthen Crown Court, an event took place of the greatest importance in the history of the Welsh language in the second half of the twentieth century. Gwynfor Evans, president of Plaid Cymru, announced that he would begin a fast to death on 6 October 1980 unless the promise to provide a Welsh-language television channel was honoured. Thousands of people had already promised not to pay for television licences and it appeared that a period of ferocious civil unrest was about to begin. Evans's model was Gandhi, who successfully used such fasting to arouse his people on six occasions. Gwynfor Evans confided to his close friend Pennar before taking the final decision to fast. Pennar supported Gwynfor's decision, justified it with his Christian belief, and even offered to join him in his fast. Gwynfor declined this offer, feeling that it would be more effective if he fasted alone.

This was followed by intense campaigning by Gwynfor Evans on the one hand and quiet diplomacy on the other by such national leaders as the Archbishop of Wales, Lord Cledwyn, the Labour senior statesman, and Sir Goronwy Daniel. The government of 'the lady's not for turning' turned, and Sianel Pedwar Cymru began broadcasting on 1 November 1982. This did not end the Davies family's worries because in September their son, Hywel Pennar, was sentenced to nine months' imprisonment for his part in the demonstrations for the Gwynfor Evans campaign. Rosemarie and Pennar had a miserable Christmas, knowing that their son was in prison, but received comfort from the large number of letters they received from well-wishers. These included one from R Tudur Jones: "Three of our children have been in prison at different times and we know well what an uncomfortable feeling it is, even when parents are in perfect sympathy with their motives and feel proud of their commitment and courage. I greatly hope that Hywel will not find this to be a nightmarish period. Our debt to him, as to you, for standing in the breach, is great indeed."[7] At last, Hywel was released and the father, like the son, found freedom.

Sadly, the house provided by the college was in poor

condition, causing even more stress to its new occupants. The ever-diligent Geoffrey Nuttall wrote on 30 July 1980: "I am distressed, fy mrawd Pennar, to read of your and Rosemarie's trials over your house and did not expect this at all. It seems very wrong that the College Council should have allowed you to go into such a house." It was a large, rambling house, chosen by Pennar and Rosemarie because they wanted enough room for all the family. It afforded panoramic views of Swansea Bay from the top of the house. Despite problems over the coming years, with Pennar's and Geraint's health problems, they did enjoy many happy years at 10 Grosvenor Road, and at a nominal rent. Rosemarie and Geraint lived there thanks to the care of Pennar Davies's late eldest son, Meirion, until 2007. However, there were many happy moments too for the family, as when they received great pleasure from the publication of a volume paying tribute to Pennar and edited by his former colleague, Dewi Eurig Davies.[8]

During the 1980s Pennar continued to produce literary material but, with a few exceptions, it lacked the importance and significance of earlier work. He addressed the United Reformed Church History Society in Bristol in 1982 on the Welsh hymn writers of the eighteenth century, a favourite theme which he had shared with Welsh-speaking students at Brecon in a series of very fine additional lectures. Nuttall cautioned him: "May I ask you to frame a little which does not sound too abstruse, peripheral or off-putting to the ignorant monoglot Englishman, otherwise I fear that your audience will be small."[9] In the summer he delivered a literary lecture at the National Eisteddfod held at Swansea, while in 1983, he delivered a lecture in Bangor on the contribution of the Welsh Independent preacher and theologian, R Ifor Parry. Then, in August of that year, Pennar and Rosemarie travelled to Switzerland as the guests and companions of Geoffrey Nuttall, who had long dreamt of taking them on an Alpine holiday.

The years of retirement, despite the freedom they brought, were not wholly comfortable. Money was scarce and there were real family problems. Geraint, who lived with his parents, had always suffered from a nervous disorder, which worsened in the 1980s. Rosemarie's mother died in 1984 and Pennar's sister, Doris May, with whom he had a close relationship, died in 1986. Apart from a few pieces and some reviews, Pennar wrote a biography of Methodist minister and writer, Tegla Davies, in the *Writers of Wales* series, but it lacked spark. What gave him particular pleasure was translating the works of poets from Switzerland, Austria and Germany into Welsh, published as *Yr Awen Almaeneg* [The German muse]. This was followed by a collection of short stories, *Llais y Durtur* [The voice of the turtle dove], most of which had been written in the 1960s and '70s, revealing his former vivacity.

At last the Welsh establishment recognised the tremendous contribution to the religious and cultural life of Wales by the man from Aberpennar. In 1987 he was created a Fellow of his old university college at Cardiff; in the following year he was the subject of a portrait film on S4C and the University of Wales awarded an honorary D.D. Pennar succeeded in publishing another volume of poetry in 1987, when he was 76 years old. Densil Morgan describes *Llef* [Voice] as the work of an old man; though it contained some good poems, its tempo had slowed down, a lack of energy could be sensed here and there and the poetic imagination was weakening.[10]

Pennar was by now well into the autumn of life. He wrote to Clem Linnenberg, his constant friend and correspondent from his time at Yale, on 3 February 1987: "At our age one looks back with mixed feelings, wondering whether we always took the right turnings." As Densil Morgan rightly points out, life could have been so different for him and his family. If he had chosen a different path he could have had a brilliant academic career, with a university chair and international acclaim, comforts for his family and time to pursue his own interests. "Instead he chose to take up the cross and to give himself utterly for the sake of Wales, the cause of Christ and the Welsh language." His choice involved lifelong sacrifice, not only for himself but for his wife and family.

Opinion is divided on the question of his choice to devote himself to writing almost wholly in Welsh. This was a deliberate decision in view of the decline of the language and the need to advance its cause and it has won the admiration of many. On the other hand, given the tremendous wealth and power of his written English, there are those, including some former Welsh-speaking students, who wonder whether he could have been a greater advocate for the cause of Christ and Wales had he chosen his first language for these purposes. His friend, Rhydwen Williams, appears to discuss this question in *Adar y Gwanwyn* [Birds of spring]. It was Pennar's decision, and his alone to make, and he did so realising that he must sacrifice the possibility of wider fame and greater reward for what he so deeply believed in.

By the 1990s it became apparent that Pennar's increasing slowness was caused by Alzheimer's disease. Although he was free of pain, the sight of his condition brought great anguish to Rosemarie, the family and his friends. In his introduction to the second edition of Pennar's spiritual classic, *Cudd fy Meiau* [Cover my sins], published in 1998, Tudur Jones wrote, "He fully realised what was happening to him. During this period he admitted that Rosemarie was now his memory." Apart from Geraint, the children had left home and were not without their own concerns but they shared a common distress at seeing their father deteriorate and the great burden this laid on their mother. Pennar celebrated his 85th birthday in November 1996. Soon afterwards he fell and was taken to hospital where he died on 29 December. So came the sad ending to a life with so much potential, which gave so much to so many and, in particular, touched the lives of generations of ministers.

17

The 'Dark' Side

THE PRINCIPAL OF Memorial College is invariably remembered
as a man of great humility and saintliness, always with a smile
on his lips, always with a kind word for his students. However,
he himself refers to the 'dark' side in *Cudd fy Meiau* [Cover
my sins][1] which first appeared as a weekly diary in the Welsh
Independent weekly, *Y Tyst*, under the nom-de-plume of the
'Brother of Low Degree' (James 1.9; A.V.), between 20 January
1955 and 16 February 1956. These writings by an unknown
minister became the focus of great interest with all sorts of
guesses being made as to the identity of the author. The late
Herbert Hughes, recently translated this work into English, and
was among the first people to guess correctly. He and I were
standing together outside the college dining room, waiting
for lunch, when he raised the question of the identity of the
Brother of Low Degree, adding that he would have been certain
it was Pennar but for the fact that one or two things did not
appear to fit with some things the principal had said to him in
conversation. At that moment Pennar himself came and joined
us. Herbert greeted him, saying, "We were just discussing the
identity of the Brother of Low Degree". Pennar burst into one
of his great smiles and said, "Oh, you have guessed!"

In *Cudd fy Meiau*, Pennar takes his readers into the inner,
secret places of his soul. He writes that "there are sexual
happenings in the life of every one of us of which we cannot
speak to our closest friends".[2] There are events and relationships
during his time in the United States which are hinted at but

never made clear but there were never more than hints as to their nature. He prays, "Lord Jesus, you forgave everything, even the Cross, forgive me the hell which burns in my heart. Let me see the humanity you intend for us, the wounds shining brightly on your body and the nature of the glory of the crown on your head, and the Flesh which was the dwelling place of the Word wrestling before me in the abundance of its delight and strength. Give me yourself, the Man who expresses God, now and for ever."[3] Other people had only the briefest glimpses of something which left them questioning, often in incidents insignificant in themselves.

Perhaps there is a hint of the 'hidden' Pennar in *Cerddi Cadwgan* (1953), in a poem entitled 'Caniadau ein Cenhedlaeth' [Songs of our generation]. Verses one and two deal with conceited girls and bosses respectively, and offer a scathing criticism of each group. The third verse is the song about the religious people and its criticism is even harsher. The original may be seen in Appendix V. A prose translation runs something like this:

> We hate to think of the state of the world;
> We prefer to sing and sing all the time.
> Because that is religion; assembly and union,
> And story and weeping and gift and cliché,
> A tearful preacher or a bishop in his pomp,
> And pilgrimages and drunken-like big meetings,
> Kissing the ring and feeding every screech,
> Mass in the morning or the service at six,
> Altar and organ and kneeling and bending,
> Looking godly and singing and singing.
> We hate to think of the state of the world;
> We prefer to sing and sing all the time.

*

Another story of Pennar's dark side came from the Carmarthen by-election of 1957. There were three candidates: Lady Megan Lloyd George (Labour), John Morgan Davies (Liberal) and Jennie Eirian Davies (Plaid Cymru). Morgan Davies, himself a Welsh Independent, wore a bowler hat, black jacket and striped trousers and always carried an umbrella. Pennar went to his home village to address one of Gwynfor's meetings and the whole village turned out to hear this famous preacher, including the Liberal candidate's sisters. Pennar asked his audience whether they really wanted "a Charlie Chaplin MP". The comment and the tone in which it was delivered caused great offence and Pennar had to write a letter of apology.

On another occasion students taking the University of Wales diploma asked me to approach Pennar who was, at that time, warden of the Guild of Graduates of the university, to seek his support in having the diploma changed into a Licentiate in Theology, with a hood. I was not prepared for his angry, scornful response and have always felt that because his impressive intellect allowed him to collect academic honours with ease, he should have been more sympathetic to students making a great effort, who wanted something to show for their endeavours. When, during my final year, I discussed with him whether I should seek ordination in a Welsh or English church because of the way my own churchmanship seemed to be moving, he pressed on me the need for pioneers in the Welsh ministry, rather than joining the ranks of those who "belonged to a mock priesthood in the English churches". I had become particularly interested in the reformed ministry and worship and was influenced by the writings of former Mansfield students. It had not occurred to me that the principal himself, in his early ministry, had shown that he had become a true 'Mansfield man' but by the mid-1950s had turned away from it, except for a spirituality which left a deep mark upon him. It should be said that when I accepted a call to a Welsh church (Wern, Aberavon, Port Talbot), he gave me full encouragement and support in my seeking to express that churchmanship at my ordination. This was the churchmanship he had imbibed at Mansfield and adopted in his ministry at Minster Road, but had now given up.

In those days it was common for a Welsh ordination to include two or even three services. I opted for the latter so as to ensure that Pennar could preach a sermon sympathetic to my aims and ideals at the actual ordination. This meant arranging two other services – one on the previous evening when my own minister, The Rev. Emrys M Jones, preached a masterly charge to the minister, followed next afternoon by a visit to the church by my predecessor, the Rev. Islwyn Davies. Pennar and everyone else leading the worship were robed, apart from the Rev. Idris Hopcyn of Cwmafan, a strict traditional Independent. Even my good friend, D Aeron Evans (sadly no longer with us), wore clerical collar and a robe. I told the principal, who also presided at the ordination, that I desired to be ordained by prayer and the laying on of hands. To this he agreed but, as he feared that it would be misunderstood, insisted that only his hands were laid on my head, whereas I had wanted Emrys M Jones, Islwyn Davies and the Wern Church Secretary, Captain George Jones, to be involved. It has always seemed to me that what I had wanted was more in keeping with the reformed tradition than what actually happened. Nonetheless I have always been grateful for his major input into the service.

There was one incident at Brecon which has continued to puzzle those students who were involved and others who've known about it ever since. The student body divided into two almost equal parts: the Larks, whose motto was "early to bed and early to rise", and the Owls, who enjoyed the hours before and after midnight. One student discovered the date of Pennar's birthday and, at one minute after midnight, the Owls gathered outside his study window to sing 'Happy Birthday'. His back door opened, and the great figure of the principal appeared in a furious rage. He demanded to know what the singers thought they were doing and ordered them to depart. There was no reference to disturbing the rest of his family or the other students. No other explanation has seemed feasible, apart from his being incensed at their crossing an invisible boundary of which they were not aware and trespassing into his privacy.

It was rare in the extreme for Pennar to lose his temper or raise his voice but, on those occasions when it happened, it deeply affected the students concerned. What is remembered by them above all else is his benign, if enigmatic smile – even at times of crisis.

18

Theology and Churchmanship

WE HAVE SEEN that Pennar Davies was brought up within the patterns of Nonconformist life and worship, based firmly on a collection of traditional dogmas, and that he underwent an evangelical conversion at the age of twelve. (He used his novel, *Anadl o'r Uchelder* [A breath from a height] to attack the distortions of crowd evangelism as he saw them.) There followed a period described by J Gwyn Griffiths as "mocking scepticism", in which he rejected all religion. This was replaced by the discovery of "a goodness, purpose and mystery in religion", which, in turn, proved of little help in the face of human evil and weakness symbolised by the causes and outbreak of war in 1939, and he discovered that the meaning of creation and humanity was centred in Jesus of Nazareth. After ordination he rejected Neo-Orthodoxy and set about finding his own interpretation of the Faith. From then on, for him life was to do with "communion with Christ, incarnate in Jesus of Nazareth. In him we meet the Pure Light of Shining Goodness. But Jesus is also the Great Disturber, whose love enslaves us, just as it sets us free." In 1949 he declared that humanity's problem is its sin and that the only answer to that sin is God's forgiveness and the new life in Christ. "Only the Cross can wake us from our deep spiritual sleep... There is no good news for the Christian if Christ is dead."[1]

Salvation is social as well as personal. "It is perfectly clear that the salvation of human society is an indispensable part of the purpose of Jesus in proclaiming his gospel and that he aimed not only at creating a 'Church' which would not only realise the Kingdom within its own society but also bring healing to the world."[2] Dr Densil Morgan comments that:

> It is an easy matter to criticise Pennar's utopianism: though he believed that man is a sinner, his ideas of the Fall are rather superficial. There is something naïve in his faith in the human potential for good. Although he acknowledges the existence of evil, he explains it as a human phenomenon rather than a reality which offends against the glory of God. (This would remove the sting of his healthy conviction about the incarnation.) He was a Pelagian who insisted that there was sufficient goodness in the human heart to be able to co-operate with the grace of God and reach perfection. But Pelagianism was a heresy condemned by the Church because it belittled the seriousness of the human spiritual crisis and thus the unique nature of the work of God in Christ. However, the strength of Pennar's position was that he challenged the orthodoxy which turned the gospel of grace into a cheap gospel, failing to take seriously the uncompromising call of Jesus to take up the cross and fulfil his work in the world.[3]

In a sermon he declared that, "The terrible thing about sin is not that it incurs God's punishment but that it misses the unimaginable joy of the people of God... God is certainly pained and outraged by our sins. He is holy, good and tender but he does not rain down death upon his children."[4] For Pennar, there is no hope apart from the Cross. Therefore the only way to find whether a theological system is truly spiritual is to ask whether it contains salvation, assuming first that humanity is in a state of sickness and crisis and secondly that God is determined to heal. He reacted strongly against those who tended to play down the Jesus of history, arguing that if Jesus is not grounded in history, then he belongs with "the saviours of the mystery religions, such as Mithras, Attic and Osiris". Theology must be based not on some doctrine about the Person of Christ but in Jesus himself, his ministry in Palestine and his saving work for us. On page 16 of *Y Brenin Alltud* [The exiled king] he writes, "I must bear my witness, in this experience of the Resurrected that I have failed completely to hear his voice claiming anything for himself: no title, no honour, no special status in history, no throne in eternity... His Divinity is made known not in strange assertions about the unique authority of his own Person but in his utter non-self seeking humility." For Pennar, Jesus claimed no unique relationship with the Father; the disciples too could experience the divine Fatherhood in his company. Jesus did not claim to be the Messiah; he became the Messiah through his death and resurrection.

When it came to the question of the Coming of the Son of Man, Pennar found himself in the same camp as biblical commentators such as T W Manson in relating the teaching of Jesus to the Book of Daniel. The followers of Jesus are both to pray for the coming of the Kingdom and to prepare its way. "Our work through the grace of God is to prepare the world to see the fulfilling of the heavenly vision, the new heaven and the new earth and, as the weakness of God is stronger than men and the foolishness of God is wiser than men, so the dream of God is truer than all the factual and theoretical knowledge of men."[5]

In a lecture on the Holy Spirit he spoke of the need to see the Incarnate Christ as the Incarnation of the Spirit as well as the Incarnation of the Word. It is the Spirit who leads us simply to the Bread of the Life. It is in the Spirit that Christ returns to his own and through his humanity his divine glory is revealed by the Spirit.[6]

As far as Pennar Davies was concerned, the Church was not an organisation but the community called to act out the power of Christian hope. He criticised those who turned churches into social clubs bearing a striking similarity to the large drinking clubs of the south Wales valleys. He attacked the religious establishment for its unwillingness to apply the Gospel to the burning questions faced by the world. "Words like Christ, Kingdom, the rule of the saints of the Most High, Son of Man are political expressions and not some small pious feelings – a complete commitment for the true Christian to enthrone the Prince of Peace above the praise of humanity."[7]

Later, "The Church is to create a revolution to conquer the world. Jesus's first sermon at Nazareth sets out a powerful social concern and the New Testament testifies that the Kingdom of Jesus is a challenge to the governments of the Roman world. Jesus, the Great Disturber, creates a dangerous radicalism, a wonderful campaign for justice and peace and an idealistic adventure to enthrone the Love of Christ. It is he who creates the revolution to overthrow the old order, the revolution of the Lord's Prayer and the movement to turn the world upside down."[8]

Within the Church itself the ordained ministry is the greatest adventure in life, possessing a splendour which is undiminished by the unworthiness of both saints and ministers. Being allowed to preach the Love of God, to preach the Cross was a sublime honour. For this college principal it was a source of pride to greet a young minister with a heart full of prophetic fire. His elevation of preaching led him to bitterly regret the danger of sin for the preacher in preparing sermons to please his congregation and accepting the resulting flatteries. He himself often felt like a voice in the wilderness when a congregation gave him a polite hearing but then turned at once to talk of the chapel's heating system or the latest news in fashion or sport.

Pennar was an ecumenist but his ecumenism was centred on the Church as a community of Christians, rather than a movement to unite denominations. He saw the need for every jot of love in order to arbitrate with grace in situations where increasingly theological divisions troubled denominations. His longing for unity was balanced by a fear of uniformity. The basis for both unity and renewal lay in meeting Jesus, who gave everything and claimed nothing, the One who is greater than all the systems in which we seek to enclose him.

As Others Saw Him

The Rev. Professor D Densil Morgan

(Baptist Minister, Head of the School of Theology, Religion and Islamic Studies, University of Wales Trinity St David; author of Pennar Davies's official Welsh biography)

It is hardly likely that the Christianity of Wales has – and certainly the Nonconformist ministry has not had – anyone in the twentieth century who was more strikingly creative, erudite and civilised than Pennar Davies. As a theologian and historian, writer of short stories and novels, literary critic and poet, political radical and mystic, and one who meditated long and extensively on the nature of the relationship of the spirit and the flesh, he was unique in the history of our recent Christianity. He possessed an enigmatic genius, which caused him to be placed somewhat apart by the literary and academic institutions despite the fact that he consecrated his extensive gifts throughout his life at the service of literature, religion and education. Like his Christ, he preferred to fulfil his callings obediently alone rather than seek worldly praise and honour. It was not an inverted boasting which led him both to adopt the name of the 'Brother of Low Degree' in that most memorable of his books and to write 'The Saviour's Servant' on the cover of one of his novels. Pennar himself was like the chief character in that novel: "His chief honour was to be the servant of that Saviour and to be, in the intensity of his service, to share in his sacrifice and hope."[1] He was, without any doubt, a faithful servant to the Exiled King.

The Rev. Dr Vivian Jones

(Coleg Bala-Bangor, 1948–55; Minister of Welsh Independent and American Congregational churches)

When I enrolled as a student at Bala-Bangor Independent College in 1948, Pennar had been installed as Vice-Principal and Professor of Church History and as Professor of Church History at the School of Theology of University College of Wales, Bangor two years earlier. He left Bangor in 1950 to become a professor at the Memorial College, Brecon.

During that brief stay at Bangor he was regarded by the students as a benign and very remarkable presence. He certainly didn't fit any preconceived ideas we might have had of a theological professor. Rumour had it that there had been concerns amongst some about his appointment; concerns centred on the fact that he belonged to an avant-garde group of Welsh-language literati. He had published a book of poetry entitled *Cinio'r Cythraul* [The devil's dinner] that included the line (my translation), "Would that I were a drop of sweat running down my loved one's back..." Such boldness could hardly not endear him to his students! Some of his idiosyncrasies were also noteworthy. On alternate days both the principal and the vice-principal of Bala-Bangor joined the students for breakfast and Pennar would turn up now and then with his suit worn over his pyjamas, the sleeves of which peeped out from under the sleeves of his suit.

Pennar's distinguished academic accomplishments were very impressive, but it was other accomplishments of his that provoked in us the greatest wonder. Kippers were a frequent item on the breakfast menu at Bala-Bangor and, when the meal was over and done with, every student's plate would be littered with fish bones, but Pennar's plate would be clean, without even a back-bone in sight!

This large, ambling, respectful, youngish professor was also an easy and friendly soul, comfortable with himself and with the students. He would invariably greet one of the senior students by asking him about his girlfriend, "How's Rosie, Dick?" and when it was his turn at the sermon class to criticise the student preacher for that day, his remarks would be significant but also generous.

There was to his scholarship and his personality a breadth which, to those of us striving to cut free from the inhibitions of the Welsh nonconformity of that time, was liberating and challenging, but there was nothing coercive about his influence. Some students left the college as replicas of Principal Gwilym Bowyer in their preaching style – a style that remained with some of them throughout their lives. But Pennar's effect on us was more subtle and pervasive, more to do with his universal acceptance of us all and with his open and affable and free attitude to life, than with specific, assertive characteristics.

Pennar seemed to have no preconceived ideas about what precisely a minister should be, let alone fixed ideas about whom or what any one of us should be. His expansive presence was an invitation and permission for us to be who we wanted to be, without criticism, let alone condemnation. As vice-principal, he wasn't, of course, in ultimate charge of the students or the college, and so was free to be who he was. How he would have related to us had he been principal would be another story perhaps. But, as matters were, had some of us been pressed to name someone that we actually knew as a saint, Pennar's name might well have sprung to mind. This, for students, a hugely significant fact in a Christian teacher, which could easily transcend any assessment of him in traditional, dogmatic ways.

Mrs Margot Morgan

(Margot Morgan is the daughter of the late Rev. Lionel T Walker (Memorial College, Brecon, 1954–7) and Mrs Bette Walker, now of Easton, Pennsylvania. When her parents returned to the United States she lived with Pennar Davies's family for eighteen months)

The eighteen months I lived as part of the Pennar and Rosemarie Davies household were of nurture and relief from the hustle and bustle of my hitherto tumultuous teenage years. I had just wasted a very unprofitable year at university in the USA, where my family lived after emigrating from Swansea, south Wales – just before my sixth birthday. I was now eighteen and my father's sabbatical in 1978 had been an opportunity for him and my mother to bring the family back to the UK for a visit. Part of that time was spent reconnecting with Pennar, Rosemarie and their wonderfully full lives in a house that seemed to me to be brimming with happy children and activity. The Pennars and my parents had been very close before the birth of my elder brother and exchanged letters and phone calls across the years. As I grew up I would dream of the rooms of the Coleg Coffa where my father studied, often taking us children with him on a visit, or sometimes we would go with my mother to see Rosemarie, or Mutti as we knew her, or to babysit. My return to that warm and loving family environment as a young and confused adult was just what I needed, and when I was invited to stay on and given the opportunity to study theology, I embraced the chance.

I did what I could to help with the myriad chores that running a big family demanded, appreciating the pressure that feeding another mouth brings, but I was always welcomed and cared for in the best way. Pennar was certainly a head-in-the-clouds type of man but it seemed to me that he always had time to be a loving and engaged father, who was adored by his wife, children, students and friends. It was a very traditional family in that Mutti did all the housework and cooking, whilst Pennar worked long hours in his study and taught and preached, often travelling for miles to visit churches around Wales. Sometimes he would take me with him and we would talk the whole way there and back – politics, religion, racism, science, history, current affairs and Wales – not just Pennar talking and me listening but real conversations, because he was genuinely interested in people and the world, and wanted to share the experiences of others. Rosemarie was also interested in every subject you wished to discuss and we shared a love of cooking and orderliness and caring. She took great loving pride in the well-being of all, spoiling us whenever the opportunity arose. Theirs was a close family and, taken into the heart of it, I thrived. They offered a foothold to a floundering teen and I will never forget their intelligence, generosity and love.

The Rev. Dewi Lloyd Lewis

(Memorial College, Brecon, 1955–8. Welsh Independent Minister)

Principal, Professor, Cymro. In the 1950s theological colleges were largely Victorian top-down institutions. Pennar Davies consciously endevoured to place student priorities centre-stage, even when they assailed the place with a strike. In the lecture room, Church History became a scholarly journey through fierce controversies calmly elucidated. In the Sermon Class student efforts were guided, nourished and even encouraged – sometimes more than the presentation merited. There is a puzzle: this giant, with deep discerning devotion to the Risen Christ, seeing his beloved Cymru struggling ever so, yet he and others somehow did nothing to initiate an Iona or Taizé-like focus for possible recovery.

The Rev. Malcolm D Page

(Memorial College, Brecon, 1956–9. United Reformed Church Minister, d. 2010)

Through three years at Brecon I saw Pennar as a family man, a teacher and a friend. He was a brother who loved us, a teacher who taught us to see God's love everywhere and towards everyone.

The Rev. Herbert D Hughes

(Memorial College, Brecon, 1952–5; held Welsh Independent and United Reformed Church pastorates; Principal Lecturer in Religious Studies, Trinity College, Carmarthen; translated Cudd fy Meiau, *Pennar's spiritual classic into English; d. 2011)*

Students are not known for appreciating their tutors. It is only later that many of Pennar Davies's students came to comprehend his true greatness and achievements. But his own personality – shy, enigmatic, patient, tolerant, peace-loving – did not further a better understanding of him. What I recall is his genial smile, his chuckle and his deep humility. (This did not in any way prevent him from standing for Parliament or breaking the law in defence of the Welsh language.) It could be considered a weakness in a principal to be humble but, on looking back, one can see that his respect for others in Christ outweighed any negative opinions he might hold of them. One can catalogue his brilliance in so many fields but at the centre of his life remained this passion for Indestructible Love, which he struggled to retain throughout his life. He was a genius and a gentleman who had great inner strength. But I shall always remember him for his smile and warmth and I shall always respect his total commitment to Christ.

The Rev. Derwyn Morris Jones

(Bala-Bangor, 1953–9, Welsh Independent Minister; General Secretary and President of Union of Welsh Independents)

The range of his scholarship and literary gifts was amazing – novelist, poet, short story writer, literary critic, historian and theologian. His *Cudd fy Meiau*, published like most of his work, in Welsh, is a classic of its kind and deserves a wider readership. It is good to know that Herbert Hughes has undertaken this task. I shall always remember the privilege we shared as Welsh Congregational ministers when he spoke to us of his spiritual pilgrimage. Many will recall his prophetic and challenging presidential address at our union meetings in 1973, under the title, 'Y Pethau nad Ydynt' [The things that are not] a phrase found in 1 Corinthians 1.29. This is one of the greatest utterances made from the Chair of the Union of Welsh Independents.

The Rev. Dr John Morgans, OBE

(Memorial College, Swansea, 1960–3; United Reformed Church Minister; Moderator, Wales Synod; President, Council of Churches for Wales)

It was a privilege to be a student of Pennar Davies from 1960 to 1963 while I was at Coleg Coffa in Swansea. I was one of nearly 40 students training for the ministry. My memories are of Pennar: living 'above the shop' and caring for his family; being at morning prayers where Pennar reflected a presence of the Risen Christ; lectures in Church History, in which Pennar reflected a quiet masterly authority of the subject, and occasionally expressed his passion for the subject. In a specialist course on Puritanism, he was meticulous in detail and reflected his love for Welsh Puritanism. I am particularly grateful for Pennar's suggestion that I should study William Erbery, the early Puritan leader. Pennar preached at my ordination in Llanidloes because Alwyn Charles, the minister who had encouraged me to enter the ministry, was caught in the snows on the Llanberis Pass. It was typical of Pennar that there were no histrionics but he simply met the need of the moment. In later years we served together on the Synod Ministerial Committee of the United Reformed Church, and always showed a deep concern for each candidate and student, always looking for that which was best in each person. Pennar always quietly expressed his love for the heritage of Wales and was passionately concerned that this should be reflected in the mission of the Church. Like most people, although I was a student of Pennar's, I wish I could have known him better, but it was sufficient to feel that he knew me, respected me and cared deeply about me – as he did for everyone he met. That was enough. Did I know Dr Pennar Davies? Yes I did and I didn't. Did Pennar Davies know me? Most certainly, and for that I am profoundly grateful.

And his minister The Rev. Dr Noel Davies, OBE

(Mansfield, 1965–8; Welsh Independent Minister; General Secretary, Council of Churches for Wales and Cytûn (Churches Together in Wales) 1977–98; Training Officer, Union of Welsh Independents; Lecturer, Trinity College, Carmarthen and University of Wales, Cardiff; Pennar's minister in his last years)

'A prolific writer; he combined in his poetry and prose a polymathic command of language, theology and psychology with a personal tenderness rooted in his Christian faith' – Meic Stephens in *The Independent*. He was constantly pushing the boundaries, not only of the imagination but also of words and images and forms, often creating words when conventional vocabulary failed. He was a natural ecumenist but had little interest in structured unity. He was a natural catholic – embracing the worldwide church – but was deeply rooted in the Nonconformist tradition. He was constantly exploring the limits of believing in the twentieth century. Some adjudged that he went beyond the limits of 'orthodox' faith. He rejected the transcendence of God ('our God is not a distancing God') and embraced the miraculous ('the unspeakable miracle of the living God, the miracle of resurrection'). As someone who spent almost his entire ministry preparing people for Christian ministry, in one essential sense, Pennar himself, and not his polymathic learning, was the greatest influence. The final sentence is the words of his former minister F M Jones in his funeral: "We shall continue to wonder. And he will continue to smile upon us."

2 0

Postscript

AND MY OWN final words written by one who had at least as much to do with Dr Pennar during my student years at Memorial College (1953–6) as any of my contemporaries, and was involved in the student strike. The articles in the Welsh Independents' weekly, *Y Tyst*, written by the Brother of Low Degree and later published as *Cudd fy Meiau*, revealed aspects of Pennar, hitherto unguessed at by those who knew him, whilst Professor Densil Morgan's magnificent biography has shared with Welsh readers many facts and aspects of his life and character hitherto hidden from the gaze of others.

Pennar was a big man, physically as well as intellectually and spiritually. His humility was ever present. I recall taking for him a telephone message that a young man from Llanwrtyd was interested in coming to college. "Oh, dear," responded Pennar, "How can I find time to go and see him?" When I reminded him that he was the college principal and that he could ask the young man to come to him, he replied in surprise, "Oh, I hadn't thought of that". He always came to his classes or among his students on other occasions with a smile and a kindly word.

On thinking back I have realised that although he shared his gifts and insights with remarkable generosity, he shared little knowledge of himself. During the strike he walked a lonely road, finding himself between a united and rebellious student body on the one side and the senate and college committees on the other. It was quite clear to the students that it was through

Pennar's eirenic efforts that the dispute came to an end and that the desire of some to punish those regarded as ringleaders came to nothing. It is worth noting that, with two exceptions, there is no reference to his everyday work in his spiritual diary, *Cudd fy Meiau*. The first records the ordination of a student of rather extreme views: "Blessing on a young minister. The Spirit lead him beyond every obscurantism and false gospel at the Truth. There are plenty of swamps and mud on the way." The other is his comments on the strike period. On 15 November he wrote:

> I have not said much about my work in this diary. It is impossible to give public detail to the joys and sorrows of the particular ministry entrusted to me... My work is an important part of my life and many of my 'spiritual' experiences are linked with the lives which touch mine as a result of the responsibility placed upon me. Today I am compelled to look with amazement at the fact that my work can fail, and fail tragically. I think of my work mainly as a pastorate in a community of Christians preparing themselves for the responsibility of leading their fellow Christians in the general ministry... I am a minister, a servant, not a master. 'Minister' not 'Magister'. This means that I serve the brotherhood and that our living together should be different from the kind of society found in a secular college. I have tried to encourage the brothers along this road, without quarreling or partisanship. It has been obvious that some have misunderstood both my methods and my aims and my feeling until today has been that we are moving in the right direction. But today there has been an explosion and the vehicle has been shaken up.

On the 16 November he wrote:

> Dies Irae everywhere. There is no escape from the lancets. O Lord, have mercy on us. You are the Minister from whom all ministries are named in heaven and on earth. Minister to us in this affliction and always. Amen. There is a glimmer of hope.

These words were published some months later but he hid his own agony behind his smiling face as he cared for his students and, doubtless, for his fellow members of the senate as well.

For my part, I can only remember him with enhanced respect for this scholarly and caring minister of Christ and increased affection for this loving man of God.

APPENDIX I

'Cathl i'r Almonwydden'

[A hymn to the almond tree]

An Introduction by Professor M Wynn Thomas

Pelagius was Pennar Davies's hero. Against St Augustine's gloomy condemnation of nature as utterly depraved, the early Christian theologian argued that the potential for enhancement by grace was already inherent in all natural forms, thus asserting a continuity between the 'fallen' and the 'redeemed' worlds. Or, as Pennar approvingly put it: 'Grace for him was not merely a remedial intervention necessitated by the Fall: it danced in the activity of the creation itself.'

'Cathl i'r Almonwydden' (to give it its original title) is a rapturous celebration of this 'dance'. While it means 'song', 'cathl' is a somewhat antique and elevated word deliberately chosen for its spiritual, sacramental associations. The poem is a joyously formal ritual of language. It invokes the wondrous blooming of the tree that signifies the revelatory reawakening of the whole world to the reckless glory of its aliveness. Hence the climactic conclusion of each stanza with an extravagant profusion of adjectives that interact to suggest the headlong, heady, yet sober, paradox of existence.

In the almond tree is, of course, figured the intoxicating paradox that, for Pennar, was the mystery of Christ's sacrifice, in which he found the key to human suffering. But it also consciously recalls, and celebrates, the dionysiac 'pagan' festival of spring, because, following Pelagius, Pennar believed that the fleshly, sensuous and sexual human body, as well as the body of nature, was instinct with divinity. Hence the opening invocation of 'many-breasted nature'. And this passion for 'paganism' is woven into the fabric of the whole poem through the many references to figures from classical and Welsh myths and legends, all of whom seemed to Pennar to pre-figure Christian truths, just as the character of the redeemed world was already adumbrated in unredeemed nature.

'The road of excess leads to the palace of wisdom', Blake memorably wrote. Pennar's poem is keyed to this belief. Ecstasy alone allows us to 'stand outside ourselves', as the Latin components of the word (ex-stasis) suggest. When 'transported' we are, indeed, carried beyond the realms of the mundane and the banal to an entirely different plane, even though in one sense everything remains exactly as before.

In its handling of language, image and rhythm, 'Cathl i'r Almonwydden' is ludic to its very core, reminiscent of Hasidic priests who have been known to get up from their deathbed to dance before the Lord. It is a jubilant poem, if we recall that, as Denise Levertov (whose own father was of Hasidic background) wrote: "Jubilation... goes back / to 'a cry of joy or woe' or to 'echoic/ iu of wonder.'" And it is the transformation of woe into joy that is the generative paradox of this altogether 'wonder-full' poem.

A Note by Owain Pennar

'Cathl i'r Almonwydden' was originally published in Pennar Davies's volume of poetry *Yr Efrydd o Lyn Cynon* in 1961. The poem has kindly been translated by the poet and translator Elin ap Hywel. The poem is regarded as one of Pennar Davies's greatest works. In his introduction, Professor M Wynn Thomas of Swansea University explains why the poem is so important in understanding Pennar Davies's life philosophy and theology. The family and the author of this biography would like to thank both Elin ap Hywel and M Wynn Thomas for their contributions.

A Hymn to the Almond Tree

(Written originally in Welsh by Pennar Davies, translated by Elin ap Hywel)

I love the fringes of many-breasted nature
And love her now, yes, more than I did before;
For I have gazed, like Brendan, on her waves
And, like Elijah, on her wind and fire;
With Math and Gwydion, have seen her hillside flowers
Amazed, transform themselves to drunk Blodeuwedd's form;
With Daphne, seen the branches from the thickets
Sustain the widowed and the weak in grief;
And I can see an almond tree
Waving her passionate whiteness to the sky,
This bold, brave tree, this gentle, laughing cross.

Over my soul there broke a wave of gladness;
I saw the Lion overleap the Sun;
The shout became a prayer, each separate sighing
A song of praise for Order, and its Price,
Became a psalm of thanks for having succoured
Rachel's heartbroken keening for her clan;
Became the triumph shout of Heledd's outcry
For generous Pengwern, for harpstring and for hearth;
For I have seen an almond tree,
A crown of shining snow upon her head,
This humble, eloquent tree, this merry, mischievous cross.

I saw the lamb that earlier was slaughtered
Skip over the earth's horizon, dying, to live again.
Paolo and Francesca's moans become a hallowed, joyful
Prancing for the Order, and its Price.
I have experienced in the cruellest winter
The daffodil growing, the budding of the rose,

Walked hand in hand with summer, drunk with the harvest sun,
Listened with others to the bees' twilight hum.
For I have seen an almond tree –
And in the temple of this world, the tearing of the veil –
This strong and silly tree, this shy and shameless cross.

O Christ, alas, each memory of your suffering
Comes as a merry tune to comfort me.
The noisome stench which rose up to your nostrils
As the most glorious incense in the world;
For I have seen a serpent sweetly coil his body
Around the Tree of Life above the flood
And heard your Dove enact your promise
With everlasting, ever glorious song
Yes, I have seen an almond tree,
Her fine and impudent top, her snowy crown,
This bold, brave, tree, this sweet, proud-laden cross.

What miracle has transformed a broken body
Into a milk-white, fertile foam of joy?
Surely the same as gave the doe her gladness,
The swallow her ecstasy under an azure sky?
Surely the miracle which turned the sane to madness?
Grey disappointment to lovely, living verse?
Surely the miracle which bewitched ancient temples
On bright slopes underneath the emerald sea?
Hail, almond tree;
Raise high your blossom to vanquish satire and shame,
This tree which hides her scar, this reckless, living cross.

Andreas Meirion Pennar
1944–2010

MEIRION, THE FIRST of Pennar and Rosemarie's five children, was born in Cardiff on Christmas Eve 1944. At the 8 a.m. Christmas Communion at the Minster Road Church, the minister and new father called the congregation to worship with the words, "Unto us a child is born, unto us a son in given".

Less than two years later the family moved to Bangor and thence to Brecon in 1950, where it resided until a final move to Swansea in 1959. Meirion spent his last three years of schooling at Dynevor Boys' School. These moves appear to have had little effect on his education as he graduated with a good honours degree in Welsh from the University of Wales, Swansea, before proceeding to Jesus College, Oxford, where he was awarded his D.Phil. in 1975 for his thesis 'Women in Mediaeval Welsh Literature: an examination of some literary attitudes before 1500'. After leaving Oxford, Meirion spent the academic year of 1969/70 working as a researcher on a national project established at the Education Department of University College Swansea, measuring attitudes to the two languages of Wales, and their influence on attainment in English and Welsh in schools. At the end of the year he left to take up a lecturing post in Dublin. In 1975 he returned to become a lecturer at the Welsh Department of St David's University College, Lampeter, from which he retired in 1994 on health grounds. Whilst in Dublin he had married Carmen Gahan and had one son, Gwri Pennar. The marriage was later dissolved during their time at Lampeter. He remained in Ceredigion for many years, living in several places, including Llandysul and Adpar, Newcastle Emlyn.

Meirion claimed to have had "an unliterary upbringing", but it is clear that the poetry bug did not bite him until he reached the sixth form at Dynevor. He published two volumes of poetry: *Syndod y Sêr* [The stars' amazement] (1971) and *Pair Dadeni* [Cauldron of rebirth] (1977) together with two long poems, 'Saga' (1972) and 'Y Gadwyn' [The chain] (1976). He was greatly influenced by German and French expressionist poets and his avant-garde verse was not to every critic's taste, owing to its complexity of expression and wealth of literary allusions. Although possible harking back to an earlier poetic artistic style, it was challenging to Welsh readers brought up on traditional Welsh metric poetry.

His articles on a broad range of themes relating to Welsh literature, appeared in a number of periodicals and magazines. It is likely that he will be remembered most of all for his translation into English of some of the important early works in Welsh literature, *Taliesin Poems* (1988), *The Poems of Taliesin*, *The Black Book of Carmarthen* (1989) and *Peredur, Arthurian Romance from the Mabinogion* (1991), are all still in print. He and Nicholas Parry published *Cad Goddau* [The battle of the trees] in 1992. Visitors to Carmarthen's new market can read on its wall a quotation from Meirion's translation of *The Black Book of Carmarthen*. His study of such works and especially the Mabinogi had a marked effect on his writings and his outlook.

His autobiographical poem, 'Ceinciau Mabinogi' [Mabinogi branches] speaks of "a youth in the grasp of his nation" and, certainly, in the 1970s and '80s he was much involved in the Welsh political struggles of that period. In 1983 he was the Plaid Cymru candidate for Swansea West, thus following in the footsteps of his father, who twice contested the Llanelli seat. Like his father, he wrote for the Plaid's Welsh newspaper, *Y Ddraig Goch* [Red Dragon]. He was an active member of the Welsh Language Society, campaigning for a more central place for the Welsh language in the life of the nation.

Following on the death of his father, at the age of 85 in December 1996, Meirion returned to the family home in Swansea to give loving care to his mother Rosemarie (1917–2010) and brother Geraint. He stayed with his son Gwri at his south London flat for several months when undergoing surgery and treatment at a London hospital, before returning to his home in Brynmill, Swansea, where he died 9 December 2010.

It is said that of the five children, it was Meirion who inherited his father's academic interests, and it was he who spent time with his polymath father discussing literature and other intriguing subjects. As has been noted, father and son shared a cultural and political commitment, which expressed itself in similar ways, whilst the academic prowess of the father was reflected in that of the son.

Meirion possessed a vivid imagination and immersed himself in early Welsh writings. He was not content just to study the Mabinogi but sought to identify with some of its characters. In this closely-knit family it was the eldest child that remained the youngest-at-heart, as brother Owain's poem suggests, living in a constant tension between a childlike pleasure and the illness which haunted him for much of his later life.

> Your half empty glasses were filled…
> your stormy, rowdy mind,
>   was a refuge for the spirit's hopes as well
> and a boylike wonder in your eyes
> when gazing at the stars.

The real world's wheel
turned cruelly for you at times
but the mind's cauldron of rebirth
kept our land's old tales
lively and young
in your writing.

Lines from 'I Meirion, fy mrawd hyna"
[To Meirion, my eldest brother]
Owain Pennar

Two Novelists and Two Novels

RHYDWEN WILLIAMS'S NOVEL *Adar y Gwanwyn* [Birds of spring] reveals the response of Pennar's close friends in *Cylch Cadwgan* to his announcement that he was to train for the ministry – but that is not all. Rhydwen's work was the second to be based on this circle of friends. It was predated by Pennar's own novel *Mab Daragon*, which was essentially a portrait of *Cylch Cadwgan* and its members. The prominent character, Eurof, was based on Rhydwen Williams and this was clearly seen by Rhydwen himself and by other readers, whereas Neddwyn *appears* to be Pennar. Rhydwen was at this time the minister of a strongly evangelical church, perhaps even of Pentecostal tendencies, in the Rhondda. He was forced to admit to himself that he did not avow the same beliefs as his congregation.

Mab Darogan [Son of foreboding] (1968)

Pennar Davies's novel begins with the portrayal of Eurof: "Eurof knew that he could put sufficient sympathy into his voice to convince everyone. Being an actor by ability and instinct was both a blessing and a curse. By his winning charm, warm tenderness and ready affectionateness he created, without fail, a favourable first impression on everyone. The evil was that everyone expected too much of him and were disappointed." (p.7)

On another occasion he attacks Eurof's sermons: "But there was no consistency in Eurof. In another sermon he could beat a completely different drum and present a message which would warm the heart of every humanist, liberal and progressive. And it was doubtful as to whether Eurof had heard anything of the New Orthodoxy, Biblical Existentialism and Crisis Theology, those exciting movements which gave him such stimulus... Neddwyn felt that the power of his (Eurof's) eloquence was lost in mere rhetoric. No, there was little substance in the talking about sin in this sermon: Eurof was just echoing the evangelical manner of the past, He had no real awareness of sin." (pp.80–1)

Rhydwen was, to say the least, unhappy with this portrayal and this was no surprise. Four years later, he counter-attacked with his own novel, also based on *Cylch Cadwgan* and its members, and with large sections based on Pennar. It is not for this observer to comment on whether or not *Mab Darogan* is another example of the 'dark side' in the character of its author.

Adar y Gwanwyn [Birds of spring] (1972)

Rhydwen Williams's novel has characters which are also based on the members of *Cylch Cadwgan*. Mr Heini Gruffudd, son of J Gwyn Griffiths and Käthe Bosse Griffiths, kindly lent me his father's copy of the book, suggesting that, although this is a work of fiction, it provides a reliable picture of all four characters significant to this article. On the last page is written a list of the characters and the people whom they match: Iwan Owen – Rhydwen Williams; Rhymni Morgan – Pennar Davies; Garmon – J Gwyn Griffiths; Elsa – Käthe Bosse; Teyrnon – David Griffiths.

*

Page 28: records Rhymni's arrival at the home of Garmon and Elsa, where Iwan has arrived earlier. Iwan is a theological student who has been living as a tramp since refusing to register for National Service. It is early in World War II. They occupy twin beds in the small front room; Iwan has already retired for the night when Rhymni arrives and prepares himself for bed. We are told that it is Garmon and Elsa who suggested that Jac Morgan add Rhymni to his name, having been known in college as 'Morgan Rhymni'. Rhymni, who gained his doctorate, has recently returned from Canada. Iwan enquiries about his future plans:

"What's the future to be, Rhymni?"

"That depends."

"On what?"

"Not on what; but – *on whom*."

"On whom?"

"The Holy Spirit."

Iwan searched in the dark for the lamp. He pointed the lamp at the face of his friend. *"What did you say?"*

Rhymni was undressing and preparing to go to the empty bed. He answered perfectly normally as though he were speaking about the weather:

"The Holy Spirit."

This quiet statement made Iwan feel uncomfortable. Worse than that: almost unclean! Rhymni had made him feel small... simple... unimportant... a number of times. This was the first time for him to make Iwan feel like this... as he felt now. It was as though Rhymni filled the room with a new, amazing presence – even though the one and sixpenny lamp lent little light to the darkness. On his travels Iwan had heard of a soldier from Llanystumdwy who jumped into a river to save a child and when he came out of the river its filth clung to him and from then onwards the river's filth broke out in ugliness over his body."

*

Pages 29–30: "Thinking about the filth of the river clinging to the soldier's body sent shivers through him. That is how he felt now... not that Rhymni intended that... not that Rhymni was responsible for that. Before this, some kind of academic glory... intellectual greatness... the importance of a multi-talented member of the intelligentsia – that was the kind of presence that Rhymni possessed. But after hearing him say in such a self-possessed quiet way now, "The Holy Spirit", he almost felt that the other was too clean to be near him and that he was too unclean to be alongside Rhymni. This was a new and strange radiance... Inner Light? ... Spiritual splendour?... Iwan had never seen his friend Jac in this light before. To be honest he did not know how to act towards him.

"What are you trying to say, Rhymni bach?"

"Do I surprise you, Iwan?"

Chi. [Iwan is shaken because Rhymni has used the respectful plural form of 'you', whereas family and close friends address each other in the singular form]. Jac Morgan Rhymni in all the glory of his cold alpine scholarliness. Iwan could not understand how to chat in a facetious and friendly way with a creature who would one day address you as *ti* as everyone else in the group said *ti*, but on the next day would change... as though he had lost confidence... changed his mind... and he would prattle *chi chi chi chi* until the word would choke a man like a bone sticking in his throat as he ate red herrings. Of course, Welsh was probably not the language of Rhymni's home and childhood, and Iwan surmised that this was responsible for the lack of confidence in using *chi* and *ti*... that is, holding a conversation in Welsh did not come naturally to him, though he had learned to speak Welsh fluently... His Welsh left his mouth like a newspaper page from a printing machine. To be honest, Rhymni's spoken Welsh was the least attractive thing about him. Sometimes he felt like grabbing his mouth and pulling out the consonants and vowels in order to see whether there was any way in the world in which to make a Welsh-speaking Welshman out of him, rather than an automaton which knew full well where the mutations were to go, but without the inner thing of the spirit, that natural thing which causes birds to fly, the stream's water to flow, and the conversation of Huw Penffridd over a cheese sandwich to be a means of grace. Rhymni would come out every now and again with words which made his nerves shrivel in his flesh in protest: *llamsachus, bochsachus.* "What do you see in old words like those, Rhymni?" he would sometimes ask him, and he would answer happily, "Two fine words! But are you complaining?" Iwan would reply imitating an English twang, "No, I don't agree with you, by the devil. I believe that you are talking through your hat. And if you think that there is charm in those two untuneful words, then I'm telling you that you need to see a doctor to get a dose in your little ears of *irdangusaryngeigus* without delay."

"Ha, Ha, Ha!" laughed Rhymni, "and what does *irdangusaryngeigus* mean?"

"The same thing as *llamsachus, bochsachus.*"

"Ha, ha, ha!" responded the brand new doctor, "Great! Great!" But it was not his fellow poet's funny vocabulary which disturbed Iwan now so much as… "What on earth did you mean by that answer? What do you mean, Rhymni?"

"Mean?"

"By replying… as you did."

"The Holy Spirit?"

"You're making me feel like William Bryan when he heard that his mate Rhys Lewis was going to be a preacher."

"Ha, ha, ha," came the laugh once more, before the tall, young man said quietly, "It may be that the situation now is not that different. To say the least, I don't know how far I fit the character of Will Bryan but Rhys Lewis' decision to dedicate himself to the Christian ministry is my experience too."

"Yours..s..s.?"

"I decided to enter the ministry!" said Rhymni, with as little fuss as though he was saying, "I'm going to post a letter."

Hearing his friend make such an announcement was indeed a strange experience for Iwan, and if he had to articulate the simple truth in his heart, he was not sure of his reaction. It was like this: he was not sure whether he considered the ministry and preaching to be his own private territory, and for no one else, none of the company which met in the home of Garmon and Elsa anyway; and hearing Rhymni give the astounding news that he was entering the ministry was like hearing that someone was trespassing on his territory. Being unwilling was stupid, but... well, to begin, what sort of preacher would Rhymni make? Had he realised that he would have to preach two sermons a week? Had he realised that the saints would have little understanding of his academic references nor appreciate his great understanding of classical literature? No one had ever thought of him, Iwan, as anything but a preacher, but – pity for the old chap – no one in his right mind would dream of Rhymni's turning his noise towards the Kingdom of Heaven. Of course, as a personality, as a gentleman, there was no way any pulpit in Wales could get a better one than Rhymni to climb into it. Sometimes, Iwan thought that he was too docile, too naïve, too genteel, and at times he believed that he had never met a gentler creature. All one could do was pray that the churches would have enough grace and sense to appreciate that.

"To the ministry?"

"I won't be a big meetings preacher like you, of course, it's pointless to expect that – but I can be a little preacher of use in the country."

Iwan would have preferred it if his friend had not said that.

"Don't talk rubbish!"

"Rubbish?"

"Talk nonsense!"

"I'm not asking for the meaning of the word. Just doubting the word's suitability."

"If you go to preach... well, you'll be a great preacher."

"I wish that I could believe that."

Rhymni got in between the bedclothes. "The thought of preparing a sermon terrifies me."

"Terrifies?"

"Yes, indeed..."

Iwan laughed – the idea was so incredible that he decided at that moment that this posture of inferiority was all a bit of a performance put on by the sly old sophist. Not always the case, of course! Sometimes. Iwan could not at all understand this sudden decision to enter the ministry. Him! Rhymni Morgan! and his talents... and his degrees... and his enchanting personality. *A minister!* Doubtless there was within him a natural love of humanity, but – to what extent was that love completely free and unshackled? Of course, there was an old Greek poem which said,

> Love without impediment
> Is worse than going to prison;
> Pure love takes care
> All grace, without charge, without deceit.

Rhymni Morgan's love was careful love. He could smile and half-laugh between his teeth for a whole evening without condemning himself... without compromising... without contradicting himself... without committing himself one way or the other. However, this loving brother was taxing his own enlightened innocence by trying to give the impression that preparing a sermon *terrified* him. "You'll have to swop some of those big, thick books – *Ulysses* – *War and Peace* – *Sons and Lovers* – Ezra Pound – and start buying volumes of sermons. There's a wide field – *The Poet's Pulpit* – *The Sermons of [John Williams] Brynsiencyn* – Richards, Pontypridd, Dafydd Morgan, Elfed, without mentioning generations of English preachers in the *Christian World Pulpit*. It will be difficult for you to come across a hair anywhere that some star has not already combed before you, but – don't lose heart – your job in the ministry will be to learn Nonconformity's great craft – *estrange!*

The *gentle* doctor lay beneath the bedclothes and the bed shook under him and his laughter came like bubbles out of his mouth. The quiet laughter continued for some seconds.

"You don't think that the Nonconformist pulpit is over original then?"

"*Do you?*"

"I never had occasion to doubt it."

"After you start going to chapel and listening to other preachers..."

"I must make an effort to listen to preachers. I listened too much to lecturers. Do you think that is likely to be a disadvantage?"

"Damning!"

"I'm drowning before I start swimming." Sound of laughter.

"Who's your favourite preacher, Iwan?"

"I don't remember his name. He was old when he came to preach at our chapel. Very old. He had white hair and a white beard. He had little sad eyes and a little, gentle voice. Dad and Mam had invited him to our house for the day. And Dad and Mam told me about him – that he had been minister of a little chapel in Cwmhafod for almost fifty years and when the great rains came to the valley once this old preacher had saved two little children from drowning when the river broke its banks and that he had taken them home and that he was very ill and doing what he did. And when I heard the old man with white hair and a white beard and the sad little eyes and the small gentle voice say in his sermon that the Good is such a blessing that it can be reached in a world such as this except through *sacrifice* – and when I heard him speak of the almond and the flowers of the plum tree can give such beauty to the world from old crooked, withered branches – and when I heard him say how beauty is scattered through the world by a breeze's touch – and when he gave me half-a-crown at the end of the day and I had never had half-a-crown before... well, I had no difficulty in believing *every word* that *that* old man had spoken!"

"Very good!... Mmmmmm! Rhymni took seconds to think over what he had heard. (Iwan thought: Surely, my-lord has not considered that I have said something of such worth that it should hover over his head!) "That old man was more than a preacher, Iwan."

"That old man was a *great* preacher."

"A prophet!"

"More than likely!"

"His sermon reminds me of Gauguin's notes. Are you familiar with Gaugin?"

"As an artist?"

"Of course."

"I don't know anything about his notes."

"He's describing a beautiful evening in Tahiti. He's asleep in his bed. There's a girl sleeping with him, Moorea. He wakes and all he can hear is the silence of the night and his own heart beating. He sees the moon's rays filtering in through the rushes of his cabin, as beautiful as the notes of a musical instrument. He went back to sleep in the sound of the music of silence. Above his head was the tall roof of pineapple leaves – a lizard lived there. In his sleep he saw the space above his head like heaven's front door. His cabin was freedom. Outside his cabin an old, withered palm-tree looking, of all things, like a polly-parrot with its golden tail dragging in the mud. Nearby was a naked man raising his heavy axe and, as he raised it above his head, a blue scar appeared in the silver firmament, and as the bow was brought down on the old withered tree, there shot out flames of beauty from the great branches, warming the night... you made me think of that when you spoke of the old preacher."

"Interesting."

"Very interesting."

"Good night, Rhymni."

"Good night, Iwan."

Sleep was far away from Iwan but he could not continue to converse with his friend. Sometimes, for some reason, though the atmosphere was friendly and pleasant, he could not open his mouth to speak another word when chatting with Rhymni. That is exactly how he felt now. Why could the fellow not let him simply tell the story of the old preacher from Cwmhafod? Not go after some of Gauguin's autobiographical notes at the end of the story. What on earth did a piece of sermon by an old monoglot Welshman have to do with the memories of some bohemian artist like Gauguin? Nonetheless, this small incident was a classic example of the difference between the two of them. He, Iwan, was so confined to his own territory, and the brilliant brother, Rhymni, could flit from country to country with no difficulty whatsoever. O God, why did he (Iwan) not have the opportunity to nest for years in the tree of knowledge? A man felt as though he had walked about with some lameness from the cradle. In the vicinity of Rhymni a man felt as though he had been crooked. A man felt... Iwan Bach, your mate expects the Holy Spirit to call around to direct him and you want to live far away on the island of your ambition! Go to sleep! Iwan realised in the silence of the room that he had the privilege of being a friend to an uncommon soul. He had assumed that Rhymni's glory lay in his brains. He admired his powers. He had been jealous – *jealous* was the word – of his scholarship... just as though Rhymni had received more sweets than he did. Childish! But the truth was that his greatness was not to do with brains – true greatness – of the man in the next bed. His decision to enter the ministry was a disclosure of a greatness that had not dawned on him, Iwan, before. Saint Rhymni was a spiritual creature. And when he thought of his own self-confidence and his pride and his feeling of enjoyable martyrdom as a chick-preacher of Reconciliation he put his head under the clothes in very shame... He felt as though he had lain in a clean bed and stained the bed-clothes... The stain of ugly selfishness.

*

Page 36: He thought of what Elsa had said at breakfast, that her neighbours had not said a word to her from the moment she came to live next door to them. The large, fat woman living opposite had come out with the sullen words, 'For shame! For shame! For shame! Your husband living at home and earning big money in the school for doing nothing... the old damn *conshy*... and my poor, little husband in khaki, fighting for his country and the bloody Germans all after him.' (As a matter of fact her little husband was batman to an alcoholic general in the heavenly peace of Windermere and having the time of his life.)

"Thank God, I've come across little like that before," said Rhymni, seated at the table, pleasant, courteous and pure (Iwan was ready to swear that, when glancing over now and again, he saw a halo around his head). "I don't think I have had much to do with the human race for years." He laughed as he spoke the sentence... it was like a musical strain sounding like an undertone to the whole of life.

"Have you had much to do with your neighbours, Iwan?" [using the familiar form of the verb]

"Too much!"

"Is that possible?"

"Take my word for it!"

"An old woman who lived next door to us in Rhymni... She knew everything about everyone. She could forecast the weather. She could foresee deaths! She could curse as she chose. I feared her in my heart..."

"I'm afraid, Rhymni, that will be your ministry."

"What?"

"Living with neighbours."

"That will be more difficult than preparing sermons."

*

Page 37–8: Elsa looks at them both at the breakfast table: "Rhymni was really a big fish to be caught in the net by Welsh Nonconformity. It was hardly likely that Iwan ever knew of a day in his life when he was not safe in the net. Iwan's gifts were such that they would make anyone take his oath that the pulpit was the only place for him. The old friend Rhymni would need to collect one or two of handy little attributes if he was to make an effective minister..." Iwan needed to get rid of one or two of his characteristics before reaching fifty. Of course, Rhymni's career as a student had been incredible... his originality as a writer was already clear... and Elsa could not doubt for a moment (any more than Garmon) that this splendid star would not go directly into the academic world. His decision to place his gifts and talents and his scholarship on the altar of Christian ministry... well, the news was like to that of the experience when the news was whispered abroad that Saul of Tarsus had started preaching. She thought: He has plenty of personality and plenty of resources to meet the demands of any church, but – and she knew quite a lot about the close and doubting and judgmental community within some chapel walls in Wales – how would his scholastic separateness and his grammatical speech and his utter deprivation of those particular characteristics which made a preacher in the eyes of Welsh people? If the great God calls a man to a particular field, she thought, let's hope he sees fit to keep his new elect in Wales – but in an *English* church. She was not sure how easy his career would be even then...

*

Page 85: Iwan – "Pity that I can't possess the purity and innocence that is in Rhymni's character before even his mental ability and all his knowledge..."

*

Page 128: Elsa, thinking: How much influence will Rhymni have on Nonconformity in twenty years or how much influence will Nonconformity have on Rhymni? Will he be a daring poet then despite the denominational strictures or will he have compromised?

*

Page 141: "From the moment Rhymni Morgan's eyes fell on the new nurse who had come to Cwm Hyder Miners' Hospital, he knew that he had found the girl he had dreamt about before ever seeing her. Despite the present evil world, Providence had been kind and life was worth living. Maria was an Italian. Like Elsa she had been forced to flee..."

136

Parliamentary Elections in Llanelli

15 October 1964

Rt. Hon. James Griffiths Philip (Lab)	32,546 (65.9%)
Philip Alfred Maybury (Con)	6,300 (12.8%)
Esyr ap Gwilym Lewis (Lib)	6,031 (12.2%)
William Thomas Pennar Davies (PC)	3,469 (7.0%)
Robert Ernest Hitchon (Comm)	1,061 (2.1%)
Labour Majority	26,246 (53.1%)

31 March 1966

Rt. Hon. James Griffiths (Lab)	33,674 (71%)
Jeremy Charles Peel (Con)	7,733 (15.1%)
William Thomas Pennar Davies (PC)	5,132 (10.9%)
Robert Ernest Hitchon (Comm)	1,211 (8.9%)
Labour Majority	26,531 (56.3%)

In both elections the Plaid Cymru and Communist candidates forfeited their deposits.

Rt. Hon. James Griffiths (1890–1975): C.H. 1966, P.C. 1945, J.P. Hon. LLD (Wales), 1946; Born in Betws, Ammanford, son of a colliery blacksmith; brought up as a Welsh Independent; entered the mines at 13, studied at the Central Labour College. From 1925 to his election to Parliament in the 1936 by-election, he was miners' agent for the Central Anthracite Miners. Chairman of the Labour Party, 1948–9; Minister of National Insurance, 1945–50; Secretary of State for the Colonies, 1950–1; Deputy Leader of the Opposition, 1956–9; first Secretary of State for Wales, 1964–6.

Philip Alfred Maybury (b. 1929): Conservative, Llanelli, 1964. Born in Macclesfield. Journalist. Chair, Swansea East Conservative Association. Secretary, Welsh Area Council, NUJ.

Esyr ap Gwilym Lewis (b. 1926): QC 1971 MA LL.M. Liberal, Llanelli, 1964. Born in Clydach Vale, minister's son. Educated, Cambridge University. Barrister, 1951; Circuit Judge, 1984.

Robert Ernest Hitchon (b. 1933): Communist, Llanelli, 1964, 1966, 1970, 1974 (February and October), 1979, 1983. Born in Llanelli. Educated, Llanelli Technical College. Toolroom machinist. AEU Shop Steward.

Jeremy Charles Peel (b. 1934): M.A. Conservative, Llanelli, 1966. Born in Farnham, Surrey. Educated, Oxford University. Stockbroker.

Caniadau ein Cenhedlaeth

[Songs of our generation]

Mae'n gas gennym feddwl am gyflwr y byd,
Mae'n well gennym ganu a chanu o hyd.
Can's dyna yw crefydd: cymanfa ac undeb,
A stori a llefain a dawn ac ystrydeb,
Pregethwr dagreuol neu esgob mewn rhwysg,
A phererindodau a chyrddau mawr brwysg,
Rhoi cusan i'r fodrwy a phorthi pob sgrech,
Offeren y bore neu'r oedfa am chwech,
Allor ac organ, penlinio a phlygu,
Ac edrych yn dduwiol a chanu a chanu.
Mae'n gas gennym feddwl am gyflwr y byd;
Mae'n well gennym ganu a chanu o hyd.

FURTHER READING

Meic Stephens, (ed.) 'Pennar Davies' in *Artists in Wales: No.1* (Llandysul, 1971).

Geoffrey Nuttall, 'Pennar Davies', *United Reformed Church History Journal*, 1997.

Obituaries in *Y Tyst*, *The Times*, *The Independent*, etc.

Dewi Eurig Davies, *Cyfrol Deyrnged Pennar Davies* [Pennar Davies tribute volume] (Swansea, 1981).

D Densil Morgan, *Cedyrn Canrif* [Strong men of a century] (Cardiff, 2001), pp.159–218.

D Densil Morgan, *Pennar Davies* (Cardiff, 2003).

For further information on those who contested parliamentary elections in Wales, see Ivor Thomas Rees, *Welsh Hustings, 1885–2004* (Llandybie, 2005).

BIBLIOGRAPHY

English Writings: *A Bibliography of John Bale* (Oxford, 1940); *Transactions of the Oxford Bibliographical Society; Mansfield College* (Oxford, 1947); *Look You* (ed.) Plaid Cymru Pamphlet, 1948; *Episodes in the History of Brecknockshire Dissent*, (Brecon, 1957); *John Penry*, (London, 1961); 'The Meaning of Messiahship', *Expository Times*, December 1975, pp.85–7; *Edward Tegla Davies* (Cardiff, 1983); Contributions to: *Modern Welsh Poetry* (1944); *The Welsh Pattern* (1945); *Christian Confidence* (1970); *Artists in Wales* (1971); *Literature in Celtic Countries* (1971); *Presenting Saunders Lewis* (1973); *Letters* (1977).

Welsh Poetry: *Cinio'r Cythraul* [Devil's dinner] (Denbigh, 1946); *Naw Wfft* [Nine fies], (Denbigh, 1957); *Yr Efrydd o Gwm Cynon* [The cripple from Cynon valley] (Llandybie, 1961); *Y Tlws yn y Lotws* [The gem in the lotus] (Llandybie, 1966); *Llef* [Voice or cry] (Llandybie, 1987).

Welsh Theology etc: *Y Ddau Gleddyf* [The two swords] (Llandybie, 1951); *Geiriau'r Iesu* [Words of Jesus], (Swansea, 1951); *Cudd fy Meiau* [Cover my sins] (Swansea, 1952) second edition, R Tudur Jones (ed.) (Swansea, 1998); *Rhyddid and Undeb* [Freedom and union] (Llandysul, 1963); *Rhwng Chwedl a Chredo* [Between myth and creed] (Cardiff, 1963); 'Duw Ysbryd Glân' [God the Holy Spirit], Gwilym Bowyer Memorial Lecture, Swansea 1970; *Y Pethau nad Ydynt* [The things which are not] (Swansea 1973); *Y Brenin Alltud* [The exiled king] (Swansea, 1974).

Other Welsh Prose: *Saunders Lewis* (ed.) (Denbigh, 1950); *Athrawon ac Annibynwyr* [Teachers and independents] (ed.) (Swansea, 1971); *Gwynfor Evans* (biography) (Swansea, 1979).

Welsh Novels: *Anadl o'r Uchelder* [A breath from the height] (Swansea, 1958); *Meibion Daragon* [The sons of prediction] (Swansea, 1968);

Mabinogi Mwys [Ambiguous Mabinogi] (1979); *Gwas y Gwaredwr* [The Saviour's servant] (Swansea, 1991).

Welsh Stories: *Caregl Nwyf* [Chalice of vigour] (Llandybie, 1968); *Llais y Durtur* [The voice of the turtle dove] (Llandysul, 1985).

Pamphlets: *Ffederaliaeth* [Federalism] (Denbigh, 1944); *Ap* [Son of] (ed.) Plaid Cymru, 1945; *Y Gongl Fach* [The small corner] (ed.) Plaid Cymru, 1952; *Gwerth Cristnogol yr Iaith Gymraeg* [The Christian value of the Welsh language], pamphlet, 1967.

Contributions to: *Gŵyr Llên* [Men of letters], 1948; *Cenadwri'r Eglwysi Efengylaidd* [The message of the evangelical churches], 1948; *Sylfaeni Heddwch* [Foundations of peace], 1949; *Camre Cymru* [Footsteps of Wales], 1952; *Cerddi Cadwgan* [Cadwgan verse], 1953; *Problemau Beiblaidd* [Biblical problems], 1954; *Saith Ysgrif ar Grefydd* [Seven writings on religion], 1967; *Cerddi* [Poems], 1969, 1970, 1971, 1972, 1977; *Storïau '70, '72* [Stories]; *Y Chwe-degau* [The sixties], 1970; *Clywch y Beirdd* [Listen to the poets], 1971; *Gwinllan a Roddwyd* [A vineyard was given], 1972; *Storïau Awr Hamdden* [Leisure hour stories], 1974; *Saunders Lewis*, 1975; *Triongl* [Triangle], 1977; *Cerddi Prifeirdd* [Poems of the chief poets], 1977.

NOTES

CHAPTER ONE

[1] Geoffrey Nuttall, 'Pennar Davies (12 November 1911–29 December 1996): complexion oppositorum', *Journal of the United Reformed Church History Society* 5 (1997) pp.574–5. Geoffrey Fullingham Nuttall (1911–2007). Born, Colwyn Bay. Educated, Bootham School, York; Balliol and Mansfield Colleges, Oxford; Marburg University. Congregational and United Reformed Church minister, ordained 1938. Church Historian. Lecturer, Woodbrooke College, Selly Oak, 1943–5; New College, London 1945–77. Only the second Nonconformist to be awarded an Oxford D.D.

CHAPTER TWO

[1] Isaiah 51.1.

[2] Pennar Davies, 'Cân Diolch', autobiography in typescript, p.5.

[3] Ibid., p.2.

[4] Pennar Davies, Clawr Glas (2).

[5] South Pembrokeshire is sometimes known as 'Little England beyond Wales'. The Norman kings of England settled Flemings there in the 12th Century, to ensure a foothold in west Wales, in the same way as the Tudor and Stuart kings of England settled Scots and English people around Dublin and in Northern Ireland. The northern, Welsh-speaking half of the county was often referred to as 'The Welshry'.

[6] Pennar Davies papers, Darganfod Cymru.

[7] 'Cân Diolch', p.18.

[8] *Artists in Wales*, Meic Stephens (ed.), (Llandysul, 1971), p.125.

[9] Ibid., p.20.

[10] Pennar Davies papers, undated autobiographical note.

[11] Jim Driscoll (1880–1925). Born in Cardiff, one of five children,

living in great poverty. Began boxing in the south Wales boxing booths. The author was told by some of the elderly residents of Treherbert that Driscoll's career advanced when he knocked out the author's grandfather in the third round in 1905. World Lightweight Boxing Champion, 1910.

[12] Freddy Welsh (1886–1927). Born in Pontypridd. Nicknamed the 'Welsh Wizard'. World Lightweight Boxing Champion, 1925.

[13] Pennar Davies, 'Cychwyn', *Taliesin*, 63, 1988, p.31.

[14] Clawr Glas (2).

[15] 'Cân Diolch', p.2.

[16] Clawr Coch.

[17] D Densil Morgan, *Pennar Davies* (Cardiff, 2003), p.10.

[18] Given the name William Thomas by his parents, he signed his poetry and other works as 'Davies Aberpennar' in the 1940s. It was later that he added 'Pennar' to his Christian names.

[19] 'Cân Diolch', p.9.

[20] Providence closed in 1987.

[21] The Big Seat, a feature of Welsh chapels, was the place where deacons or elders sat, immediately below the pulpit. In Welsh-language churches the tradition is that they turn to face the congregation during the singing of hymns.

[22] Thomas Henry Huxley (1825–95) English biologist, described as 'Darwin's Bulldog' because of his advocacy of Darwin's Theory of Evolution. Used the term 'agnostic' to define his own attitude to theology.

CHAPTER THREE

[1] Professor J Gwyn Griffiths (1911–2004). B.A. D.Litt. Hon. D.D. (Wales) M.A. (Liverpool) D.Phil. (Oxon). Educated, Rhondda County Boys School, Porth; University of Wales, Cardiff; Queen's College, Oxford; Liverpool University. Teacher at Porth and Bala. Lecturer in Classics, University of Wales, Swansea. Noted Egyptologist. Plaid Cymru candidate for Gower, 1959, 1964. Poet and writer. Baptist lay preacher.

[2] Käthe Bosse-Griffiths (1910–98). Born in Wittenberg; partly Jewish parents but brought up as a Lutheran. Doctorate in Classics and

Egyptology (Munich). Dismissed from Berlin State Museums because of her Jewish blood. Arrived in Britain in 1936. Researcher in Egyptology, Petrie Museum, London, then Ashmolean Museum, Oxford. Keeper of Archaeology, Swansea Museum. Welsh writer and novelist.

3   Clawr Glas (1), p.7.

4   Pennar Davies papers, 'The New Wales', p.20.

5   Dame Olive Annie Wheeler (1885–1963) D.B.E. 1949, M.Sc. (Wales), Ph.D. (London). Professor of Education, UCW Cardiff, 1929–51. Labour candidate for the University of Wales, 1922. See *Who was Who 1961–70* (London, 1972).

6   Pennar Davies papers, letter dated 26 September 1934.

7   Clawr Coch.

8   Ibid.

9   Gwynfor Evans, *For the Sake of Wales* (Cardiff, 1996), p.33.

10   Gwynfor Richard Evans (1912–2005) Ll.B. (Wales) M.A. (Oxon). Secretary, Heddychwyr Cymru (Pacifists of Wales), 1939–45. President, Plaid Cymru, 1945–81. M.P. for Carmarthen, 1966–70, 1974–9. Treasurer, Union of Welsh Independents, 1964–, President. First recipient of World Wide Wales Award, 2000; Voted 'Greatest Living Statesman' in *Western Mail* poll, 2004.

CHAPTER FOUR

1   Pennar Davies papers, radio script 1943, 'An American University through the eyes of a Welshman'.

2   Haniel Long (1886–1956), son of Presbyterian missionaries; born in Rangoon, Burma. Educated, Harvard. Taught English at Pittsburg University. Settled in Santa Fe in 1929 to write. Idealist and reformer of strong religious faith.

3   Pennar Davies, *Cudd fy Meiau* [Cover my sins], a spiritual diary published in 1955.

4   In 1936 the Westminster government announced its plan to establish a bombing school at Penyberth on the Llŷn peninsula after earlier plans for sites in Northumberland and Dorset met local opposition. Half a million Welsh protests were ignored by Prime Minister Stanley Baldwin. Saunders Lewis wrote that the

British government was intent upon turning "one of the essential homes of Welsh culture, idiom and literature into a place for promoting a barbaric method of warfare". On 8 September 1936, the bombing school building was set on fire by Lewis and two other leading Welshmen, D J Williams and the Rev. Lewis Valentine, who then immediately gave themselves up to the police. A jury at Caernarfon Assizes failed to agree a verdict and the case was transferred to London's Old Bailey, where an English jury convicted them and they were sentenced to nine months imprisonment in Wormwood Scrubs. A crowd of 15,000 welcomed them back to Caernarfon. The bombing school plan was abandoned.

5   Pennar Davies papers, letter of Edith Davies, 8 March 1938.

6   Pennar Davies, unpublished diary, pp.27–8.

CHAPTER FIVE

1   Pennar Davies, unpublished diary, p.49.

2   Dewi Eurig Davies, *Cyfrol Deyrnged Pennar Davies* (Swansea, 1981), pp.9–10.

3   Clawr Coch.

4   Alun Llywelyn-Williams (1913–88) Born in Cardiff. Worked for the BBC in Cardiff and on the staff of the National Library of Wales, 1936–9. Royal Welsh Fusiliers, 1939–45. BBC programme producer, 1945–8. Director of Extramural Studies, Bangor, 1948–78. Poet, critic, writer.

5   Pennar Davies papers: letter to Alun Llywelyn-Williams, 13 August 1940.

6   Heini Gruffudd, e mail, 20 May 2011: "Käthe was my mother's name on her birth certificate. She adopted 'Kate' after coming to Wales and 'Kate' is the name on her books. The two forms are therefore correct."

7   David Robert Griffiths (1915–90). Born in Pentre, Rhondda. Baptist Minister, 1940. Lecturer in Religious Studies at English teacher training colleges, 1946–8; Lecturer, Cardiff Baptist College, 1948–55; Lecturer in Biblical Studies, UCW Cardiff, 1955–79.

8   Robert Rhydwenfro (Rhydwen) Wiliams (1916–97) Born in

Pentre, Rhondda. Conscientious Objector on nationalist grounds. Baptist minister at Ynyshir, 1941–6; Resolven, Pontlliw, then Rhyl, 1946–60. Welsh Language Presenter, Granada Television. Novelist and poet.

9   John Hughes (1896–1968) Born Rhosllannerchrugog. Organist and Choirmaster, Noddfa Baptist Church, Treorchy, 1924–42; County Music Organiser, Merioneth, 1942.

10 Arwel Hughes (1909–88) Born Rhosllannerchrugog. Joined BBC Wales's music department, 1935; Head of Music 1965–71. Organist, conductor, composer.

11 Gareth Alban Davies, son of Welsh Independent Minister, T Alban Davies; later Professor of Spanish at Leeds University.

12 Pennar Davies, in *Artists in Wales*, pp.120–9.

13 Pennar Davies papers, letter from Alun Llywelyn-Williams, 1 August 1940.

14 Letter from Gwynfor Evans, 23 September 1940.

15 Keidrych Rhys (William Ronald Rhys Jones; 1915–87). Welsh literary journalist, editor and poet. Editor of *Wales* from 1937.

16 Rhydwen Williams, *Adar y Gwanwyn* (Llandybie, 1972) (see Appendix III).

17 Nathaniel Micklem CH (1888–1976). Ordained to Congregational Ministry, 1914. Chaplain, Mansfield College, 1918–21; Professor, Selly Oak Colleges, 1921–7; Professor, Queen's College, Kingston, Ontario, 1927–31; Mansfield College, 1931–2; Principal, 1932–53. Chairman, Congregational Union of England and Wales, 1944; President, Liberal Party, 1957. Officiated at wedding of (Prime Minister) Harold Wilson and Mary Baldwin, 1940. Pioneer of Orthodox Dissent (Barthian). Ecumenist.

18 Neo-Orthodoxy: a theological movement which developed in Europe after the Great War in reaction to the theological liberalism of the previous century. It revalued the teachings of the Reformation. Associated primarily with the names of Karth Barth and Emil Brunner, it is also known as the Theology of Crisis and Dialectic Theology.

19 Cecil John Cadoux (1883–1947). Hebrew Tutor, Mansfield College, 1914–19; Minister, Benson Congregational Church,

1918–19; Professor, New Testament, Yorkshire United College, Bradford, 1919–33; Mackennal Professor of Church History and Vice-Principal, Mansfield College, 1933–47. Founder member, Fellowship of Reconciliation, 1914. "A firm liberal evangelical." (Alan Sell, *Who they were in the Reformed Churches in England and Wales, 1901–2000*, (Donnington, 2007), p.22.)

[20] R Tudur Jones, Introduction to the second edition of *Cudd fy Meiau*. 1998. Robert Tudur Jones (1921–98) B.A. B.D. D.D. Hon. D.Litt (Wales), D.Phil. (Oxon). Educated, University College of Wales, Bangor and Coleg Bala-Bangor; Mansfield College, Oxford; Strasbourg University. Ordained 1948. Welsh Independent Minister. Vice-Principal and Professor of Church History, Bala-Bangor, 1950–65; Principal, 1965–86. President, Union of Welsh Independents, 1986–7. President, Free Church Council of Wales, 1986–7. Moderator, Free Church Federal Council of England and Wales. Moderator, International Congregational Fellowship. Vice-President, Plaid Cymru. Contested Anglesey, 1959, 1964. Historian and author; books include *Congregationalism in England and Wales, 1662–1963*.

CHAPTER SIX

[1] Hans Herbert Kramm came to the UK as a liaison officer for the German Confessing Church; he founded a Lutheran congregation at Mansfield College, consisting mainly of refugees. His official reason for coming was to do a postgraduate study at the college – a thesis on Martin Luther was awarded an Oxford D.D.

[2] Eric Routley (1917–82) M.A. B.D. D.Phil. (Oxon), Ordained 1943. Lecturer, Mansfield College, 1948–59; President, Congregational Church in England and Wales, 1970–1; Visiting Professor, Princeton Theological Seminary, 1975; Professor of Church Music, Westminster Choir School, Princeton, 1978–82.

CHAPTER SEVEN

[1] Nikolaj Frederik Severin Grundtvig (1783–1872), pastor, teacher, poet, philosopher, politician. Father of modern Danish nationalism.

2 *United Reformed Church, Minster Road, Cardiff, Jubilee Booklet,* (Cardiff, 1973) p.13.

3 Sermon, 'The Mockers, the indifferent and the believers'; Acts 17. 32–4.

CHAPTER EIGHT

1 Pennar Davies, 'The Social Tradition of Christian Wales', in *The Welsh Pattern,* ed. Pennar Davies.

2 Sermon, 'Rejoice with them that rejoice'; Romans 12.15.

3 Information supplied by Heini Gruffudd, son of J Gwyn Griffiths and Käthe Bosse Griffiths.

4 Howell Elvet Lewis (1860–1953) CH 1948 Hon, M.A. D.D. LLD (Wales), minister in Welsh Independent churches. Poet and hymn writer. Chair, London Missionary Society, 1910, 1923. National President, Free Church Federal Council, 1926; Chair, Congregational Union of England and Wales, 1933. Archdruid of Wales. See *Who they were in the Reformed Churches in England and Wales, 1901–2000.*

5 Elaine Kaye, *Mansfield College, Oxford, Its Origins, History and Significance* (Oxford, 1996), p.221.

6 David Alun Lloyd (1926–2002). Ill-health prevented his entering the ministry. Teacher; then lecturer in Welsh and Drama, Trinity College, Carmarthen, 1968–74; Publicity Officer, Gwynedd County Council, 1974; Second-hand book dealer. Plaid Cymru candidate for West Flint, 1966.

7 Morgan Islwyn Lake, Welsh Independent Minister. President, Union of Welsh Independents.

8 Frederic (Deric) Morris Jones. Welsh Independent Minister. President, Union of Welsh Independents.

9 *The Welsh Pattern,* ed. Pennar Davies, (Llanmadoc, 1945).

10 Pennar Davies papers: letter to Nathaniel Micklem, 15 May 1950.

CHAPTER NINE

1 Joseph Jones (1877–1950) J.P. B.A. B.D. Hon LLD (Wales), M.A. Oxon. Educated University of Wales, Cardiff; Congregational Memorial College; Mansfield College, Oxford; Heidelberg

University. Professor New Testament, Brecon, 1907–50; Principal, 1943–57; Dean of Theology, University of Wales, 1931–4;Chair, Union of Welsh Independents, 1946–7; Moderator, Free Church Federal Council of England and Wales, 1949–50; member, Council, Congregational Union of England and Wales; Board of London Missionary Society. Liberal candidate for the University of Wales, 1923. Breconshire County Alderman. Chair, Education Committee, 31 years. An authority on the administration of education, much involved in the preparation of the Butler Education Act, 1944.

2   Pennar Davies papers, letter from Geoffrey Nuttall.

3   Published by the author, December 2010. See pages 121–3.

4   William David Davies (1911–2001). Born, Glanaman. Educated Ammanford County School; University of Wales, Cardiff; Congregational Memorial College, Brecon; Cheshunt College, Cambridge. Ordained 1942. Tutor, Cheshunt College, 1941–2; Professor of New Testament, Yorkshire Independent College, 1946–50; Duke University, Durham, North Carolina, 1950–5; Professor of Religion, Princeton University, 1955–9; Edward Robinson Professor of Biblical Theology, Union Theological Seminary and Adjunct Professor, Columbia University, 1959–66; Research Professor, Duke University, 1966–81; Professor of Religious Studies, Texas Christian University, 1981–5. Fellow, American Academy of Arts and Sciences; Corresponding Fellow, British Academy; Recipient of the Burkitt Medal, British Academy 1964; President, Society of New Testament Studies, 1976. See Robert Pope's article in *Who they were in the Reformed Churches of England and Wales 1901–2000*, pp.49–50.

5   Ieuan Davies, op.cit. p.123.

6   John Evans (c.1860–1963). Little elementary education, New College, London. Ordained in Breconshire, 1887. Minister, Glamorgan Street, Brecon, 1894–1905; Professor of Church History, Memorial College, 1905–43. Introduced the Queen's Christmas Day Broadcast. His earliest memory was of the family's eviction from their farm because his father voted Liberal in the 1868 election. The evictions in west Wales played a major part in the campaign to introduce the secret ballot.

[7] Rhys Llwyd: 'Heresi'r Pietist drwy lygaid Pennar Davies' [Pietist heresy through the eyes of Pennar Davies]; an essay which appeared for a time on Rhys Llwyd's website; adapted by the author under the new title 'Ymhél dau lenor a dwy ddinas' in *Tŷ Chwith* magazine, Vol. 29 (2008). It defines Pietism and presents Pennar's response to it, with references to Tudur Jones and Noel Gibbard. The author states that, "Doubtless it will be soon acknowledged that Christianity has had as great an influence on politics in Wales, say, as the influence of Marxism in Russia. The second half of the previous century had seen a great awakening among the Methodists and there was another substantial awakening in 1859... For a long time the Methodists were unwilling to engage in politics, believing that the Christian's primary duty was to be concerned for spiritual matters and to live a spiritual life... Though R Tudur Jones sat close to Pennar on the tarmac at Trawsfynydd that September in 1951, it must be emphasised that Tudur Jones... criticised Pietism from a position which was revolutionarily different from that of Pennar, stressing the Lordship of God rather than believing in Man's power to improve things. In closing I should like to quote Densil Morgan, who said, 'Evangelicalism divorced from radical and wholehearted social responsibility will fail and deserve to fail.' (*The Span of the Cross*, p.278.) It is likely that is the kind of response that Pennar and Tudur Jones gave to Colonel Jones-Williams... "

[8] Robert Tudur Jones (1921–98). B.A. B.D. D.D. Hon. D.Litt. (Wales) D.Phil. (Oxon). Educated, University of Wales, Bangor; Coleg Bala-Bangor; Mansfield College, Oxford; Strasbourg. Welsh Independent Minister and Church historian. Ordained, 1948. Professor of Church History, Bala-Bangor, 1950–88; Principal, 1965–88. Dean of Theology of the University of Wales, Bangor, 1978–81. Hon. Professor, Religious Studies, University of Wales, Bangor, 1990–8. Chair, International Congregational Fellowship, 1981–5. Moderator, Free Church Federal Council, 1985–6. President, Union of Welsh Independents, 1986–7. President, Free Church Council of Wales, 1986–7. Vice-President, Plaid Cymru. Parliamentary candidate for Anglesey, 1959, 1964.

9   John Daniel Vernon Lewis (1879–1970). Adopted the name 'Vernon' to distinguish himself from another student with the same name. B.A. B.D. Hon. D.D. (Wales) M.A. (Oxon). Educated University College, Cardiff; Memorial College, Brecon; Mansfield College, Oxford; University of Leipzig. Ordained 1909. Welsh Independent Minister. Professor of Theology and Ethics, Memorial College, 1934–43; Professor of Hebrew and Old Testament, 1943–57; Principal, 1950–2. Dean of Theology, University of Wales, 1949–52, Member, Royal Asiatic Society. The first person to publicise Karl Barth in Welsh.

10   David John Davies (–1976). B.A. Educated, University College, Cardiff; Memorial College, Brecon. Welsh Independent minister. Professor of Philosophy of Religion and Christian Doctrine, Memorial College. Editor of the Brecknock Society's journal, *Brycheiniog*, for many years from its inception.

CHAPTER TEN

1   David Glyn Bowen (1933–2000) B.A. B.D. (Wales) M.Th. (Princeton) Ph.D. (Leeds) Educated University College, Cardiff; Memorial College, Brecon; Princeton University. Ordained 1960. Congregational Minister at Tredegar and in Essex. Principal, Theological College, Samoa, 1963–8. Part-time minister and lecturer, London, 1968–73. Lecturer, Bradford College, 1973–99. Played a major role in inter-faith and inter-racial life in Bradford.

2   Sir George Clark Williams, 1st Bart. 1955; K.C. 1934, Hon. LLD. (Wales); 1878–1958. Barrister. National Liberal candidate for Llanelli, 1922. Lord Lieutenant of Carmarthenshire, 1945–50. Chairman, Carmarthenshire Quarter Sessions.

3   James Henry Howard (1877–1947) Descendant of John Howard, prison reformer; Orphan; Miner; Minister, Presbyterian Church of Wales, Swansea, Cwmafan, Birkenhead, Colwyn Bay, Liverpool. Noted Great War Pacifist. Labour candidate for Merioneth, 1931. See autobiography, *Winding Lanes* (Caernarfon, 1938).

CHAPTER ELEVEN

1 John Baillie (1886–1960) Church of Scotland minister; theologian and writer; professor at Edinburgh University. Moderator of the General Assembly of the Church of Scotland, 1943.

2 Canon L W Grensted, Nolloth Professor of the Christian Religion, Oxford University.

3 Rev. Dr Vincent Taylor; Methodist minister; distinguished biblical scholar.

4 Professor J R Jones (1911–70) Professor of Philosophy, Swansea 1951–70. Provided a philosophical basis for the Welsh Language Society in the 1960s. Member, Presbyterian Church of Wales.

5 Pennar Davies papers, 'Memorandum on Theological Education', 15 May 1955.

6 David Phillips Robert (1884–1966) Welsh Independent Minister. Professor of New Testament, Carmarthen, 1936–59; Swansea, 1959–64.

7 David Lewis Trefor Evans (b. 1909) Welsh Independent Minister. Professor of Old Testament, Carmarthen, 1936–59; Brecon, 1957–9; Swansea, 1959– .

8 D Densil Morgan, *Pennar Davies*, p.117.

9 Dim ond am ddyrnaid o aur y'n gadawodd,
Am ryw hen daclau i'w dangos i'r byd.
Cafodd yr hyn nad yw gennym, a thawodd.
Talodd trwy golli'n trysorau i gyd.

10 Pennar Davies papers, letter to D Gethin Williams, 12 December 1958.

CHAPTER TWELVE

1 John Saunders Lewis (1893–1983). M.A. (Liverpool) Hon. D.Litt. (Wales). Born, Liverpool, son of a Presbyterian Church of Wales minister; Converted to Roman Catholicism. Dismissed from his post as lecturer in Welsh at University of Wales, Swansea, for his part in the burning of a shed at a proposed RAF station in Lleyn in 1937. With the Rev. Lewis Valentine and Mr D J Williams tried at Caernarfonshire Assizes, where the jury failed to agree; found guilty at the Old Bailey; served sentence at Wormwood Scrubs.

Playwright and author. President, Plaid Cymru, 1928–39. Candidate for the University of Wales, 1931; 1943 by-election.

2   J Gwyn Griffiths' article, 'The Politician and Social Thinker', in *Cyfrol Deyrnged Pennar Davies* (Swansea, 1981), pp.41–51; ed. Dewi Eurig Davies.

3   Letter from R Tudur Jones to Ivor Thomas Rees, 15 August 1998: "One thing that can be asked is what motives impelled these men [i.e. ordained ministers] to take up political action. In the case of those who stood for Plaid Cymru in the 1950s and '60s, one powerful element was the persistence of Gwynfor Evans. Of course, Pennar Davies and Eurwyn Morgan (like John Gwyn Griffiths and others) were his close friends. In my own case I remember the pressure Gwynfor exerted on us to be named as candidates... On looking back, the surprising thing is that we had no political ambition. I don't know what in the world we would have done if we had won a parliamentary election."

4   See Plaid Cymru collection at National Library of Wales.

5   Sir Glanmor Williams C.B.E., F.B.A., Professor of History, University College, Swansea.

6   Europe's Dark Ages are known in Welsh as 'The age of the Saints'.

7   Rt. Hon. Thomas George Thomas was created Viscount Tonypandy by Margaret Thatcher, 1983. Teacher, Labour M.P. for Cardiff Central, 1945–50, Cardiff West, 1950–83. Secretary of State for Wales, 1968–70. Speaker of the House of Commons, 1976–83. Vice-Chairman of the Methodist Conference, 1960–1.

8   James Griffith (1890–1975), Labour M.P. for Llanelli and Cabinet Minister; Cynon: Rev. Sir Albert Evans-Jones, minister of the Presbyterian Church of Wales; Archdruid of Wales. Gwilym Ednyfed Hudson Davies (b. 1929), Labour M.P. Conwy, 1966–70; Caerphilly, 1979–83; son of the Rev. E Curig Davies, General Secretary of the Union of Welsh Independents.

9   Dic Siôn Dafydd – the name given to a Welshman who rejects his Welshness and his language (after a character in a satirical poem by Jac Glan-y-Gors).

10   Pennar Davies papers, untitled.

11   D Densil Morgan, *Pennar Davies*, p.142.

¹² Pennar Davies papers: Nathaniel Micklem to Pennar Davies, 18 August 1974.

CHAPTER THIRTEEN

1 Huw Ethall, 'Pennar Davies: Y Dyn a'i Waith', Annual Literary Lecture, National Eisteddfod of Wales, Bro Ogwr, 1998.

2 Gilbert Ruddock in *Pennar Davies Cyfrol Deyrnged*, p.55.

3 John Rowlands, Ibid., p.17.

4 Ibid. pp.17–18.

CHAPTER FOURTEEN

1 Pennar Davies papers: Gilbert Ruddock to Pennar Davies, 15 May 1971.

2 Pennar Davies papers: Crundale Congregational Church to Pennar Davies, 30 April 1971.

3 Pennar Davies papers: letter from Geoffrey Nuttall to Pennar Davies, 17 June 1970.

4 The author recalls hearing Tudur Jones, with Viscountess Stansgate, the two main speakers at an 'anti URC' fringe meeting at a Congregational Assembly in London. Whereas she often mentioned the word 'denomination', Tudur Jones insisted that Congregationalism was not a denomination but 'The People of the Way'.

5 Pennar Davies papers: letter from Geoffrey Nuttall to Pennar Davies, 9 November 1976.

6 Pennar Davies papers: mss. 'Rhagolygon wedi ymddeol' [Prospects after retirement].

CHAPTER FIFTEEN

1 Pennar Davies papers: letters from Tudur Jones to Pennar Davies, 22 January 1966 and 29 November 1966.

2 Rev. Dr Noel Gibbard, M.A. B.D. Ph.D. Trained for the Ministry at Bala-Bangor. Formerly Welsh Independent Minister at Dowlais and Llanelli. Lecturer in Theology and Church History at South Wales Bible College, Barry; President, Bryntirion Evangelical Theological College, Bridgend. Author in Welsh and English.

In the acknowledgement in his book, *Griffith Jones, Apostle to Central China* (Bridgend, 1998), Gibbard writes this of Dr Tudur Jones, "I join with others to pay my tribute to this great man. He was a scholar, historian, theologian, lecturer, essayist and a powerful preacher of the gospel. He was one of God's giants."

3   Rhys Llwyd blog 18 September 2008, *'Undodwyr yn y Coleg Coffa a Rôl Apostolaidd Dr Tudur':* "Drwy ei safiad uniongred fe fagodd Dr Tudur Jones, yn gwbl ddi-fwriad bid siwr, ddilyniant brwd ymysg efengylwyr tu mewn a thu allan i Undeb yr Annibynwyr. Deuai credinwyr o berwad Efengylaidd at Dr Tudur Jones am gyngor a dyna ddaeth i'r amlwg yn 1973 pan agorodd Pennar Davies ddrysau'r Coleg Coffa yn Abertawe i Undodwyr. Noel Gibbard, unwaith yn rhagor, oedd yn rhannu gofid gyda Dr Tudur Jones ar y mater: 'Y mae un athro a 3 myfyriwr yn Abertawe yn Undodiaid' meddai Gibbard. 'Nid yw llawer o'r eglwysi yn gwybod hyn.' Penderfynodd Noel Gibbard a'i gyd-swyddogion yn Llanedi beidio derbyn Undodwyr i'w pulpud. Mynegwyd yr un gwrthwynebiad gan Annibynwyr o berswad Efengylaidd ym Meirionydd – ysgrifennodd John a Mari Jones at Dr Tudur Jones o Lanymawddwy i fynegu braw am y myfyrwyr a ddaethai i lanw pupudau eu bro. 'Undodwr oedd yr un ddaeth atom,' adroddai John a Mari Jones gan ychwanegu fod y myfyriwr yn 'gwadu dwyfoldeb Crist'. Ymhen pythefnos cyrhaeddodd yr ail Undodwr o Abertawe ond ei anfon yn ôl at y Coleg Coffa er mwyn Esbonio eu rheswm yn blwmp ac yn blaen." Rhys Llwyd has been awarded the R Tudur Jones Memorial Scholarship at the School of Theology and Religious Studies at Bangor University as a Ph.D. student to research the life and work of Dr R Tudur Jones.

4   Rev. Iorwerth Jones, B.A. B.D. (1913–92) Welsh Independent Minister: Pant-teg, Ystalyfera, 1938–59; Capel Als, Llanelli, 1959–75; General Secretary, Union of Welsh Independents, 1975–85. Editor, *Y Dysgedydd*, *Porfeydd* and *Y Tyst*, Leading liberal thinker among the Independents.

5   Rhys Llwyd blog 11 September 2008: "Dengys y dadlau cyhoeddus rhwng RTJ ac Iorwerth Jones mae RTJ oedd ceidwad deallusol

y ffydd glasurol Efengylaidd o fewn rhengoedd Annibyniau ac Anghydffurfiaeth yn gyffredinol yn ei gyfnod."

CHAPTER SIXTEEN

1   D Densil Morgan, *Pennar Davies*, p.165.

2   Ned Thomas, *Bydoedd Cofiant Cyfnod* (Talybont, 2010), p.158.

3   Pennar Davies papers: letter from Geoffrey Nuttall to Pennar Davies, 17 November 1979.

4   Jennie Eirian Davies (1925–82). Educated Pencader Grammar School and University College of Wales. Aberystwyth. Teacher, lecturer. Editor of *Y Faner.* President, Merched y Wawr. Chair, Plaid Cymru Women's Section. Candidate for Carmarthen, 1955, 1956 by-elections.

5   Pennar Davies, Meredydd Evans and Ned Thomas, *Achos y Tri; Areithiau Llys y Goron, Caerfyrddin* (1980).

6   Pennar Davies papers, letter from Geoffrey Nuttall to Pennar Davies, 30 July 1980.

7   Pennar Davies papers, R Tudur Jones to Pennar Davies, 8 November 1980, quoted in D Densil Morgan's *Pennar Davies*, p.197.

8   Dewi Eurig Davies, *Cyfrol Deyrnged Pennar Davies* (1981).

9   Pennar Davies papers: letter Geoffrey Nuttall to Pennar Davies, 16 June 1981.

10   D Densil Morgan, *Pennar Davies*, p.178.

CHAPTER SEVENTEEN

1   *Cudd fy Meiau* [Cover my sins].

2   Pennar Davies, *Cudd fy Meiau*, 2nd edition, p.72.

3   Ibid., p.159.

CHAPTER EIGHTEEN

1   Pennar Davies, *Cudd fy Meiau*, 2nd edition, p.159.

2   Pennar Davies, *Efengyl a Chymdeithas* [The gospel and society], pp.51, 288.

3   D Densil Morgan, *Pennar Davies*, p.85.

4   Pennar Davies, sermon: 'His salvation is nigh' (Psalm 85).

5   Pennar Davies, *Y Pethau nad Ydynt*, p.17.

6   Pennar Davies, Gwilym Bowyer Memorial Lecture: 'God the Holy Spirit', 1970.

7   Pennar Davies, *Y Pethau nad Ydynt*, p.7.

8   Pennar Davies, *Y Ddau Gleddyf*, p.73. A study of the relationship between Church and State from New Testament times, drawing on his reading of texts in their original Greek, Latin, German, English and Welsh.

CHAPTER NINETEEN

1   D Densil Morgan, *Cedyrn Canrif* (Cardiff, 2001), p.158.

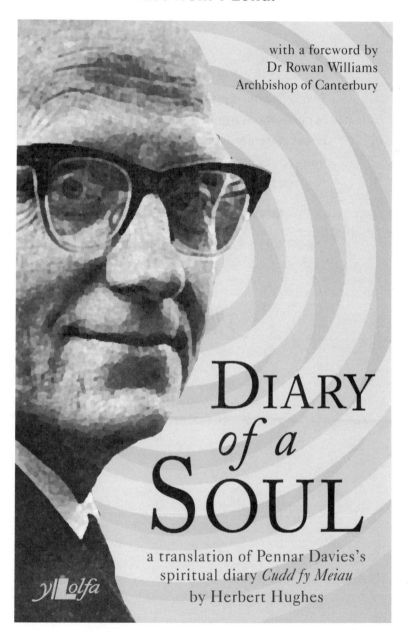

Saintly Enigma is just one of a whole range
of publications from Y Lolfa. For a full list of
books currently in print, send now for your
free copy of our new full-colour catalogue.
Or simply surf into our website

www.ylolfa.com

for secure on-line ordering.

TALYBONT CEREDIGION CYMRU SY24 5HE
e-mail ylolfa@ylolfa.com
website www.ylolfa.com
phone (01970) 832 304
fax 832 782